Productivity habits and managing procrastination

Discover new strategies to combat laziness, improve the mind and reach the goal thanks to planning and self-discipline

Table of Contents

Introduction

Answer this honestly!

Are you being the best version of yourself? Do you really believe you have accomplished everything you are capable of achieving? Do you think others have it all while you are struggling to find the secret ingredient to success, wealth, glory, and life-mastery?

Are you happy and satisfied with where your life is headed? Have you accomplished the success you deserve? Are you living the life of your dreams and visions? No! It is time for some reprogramming and transformations. You'll be blown away by how much you can accomplish by making small changes in your daily habits. Small steps go a long way in ensuring big success. These are not just theoretical, unrealistic tips on paper. This is real, actionable, practical advice that I've used to transform my own life. These are tried and tested principles used by several people to bring about a 360-degree change in their life. The pointers mentioned in this book will streamline your efforts and bring more discipline to your actions.

This in turn leads to a positive mindset geared for wealth and success. Being rich and successful begins with a mindset before you can manifest it as your reality. The pointers mentioned throughout the book can bring about amazing changes in the way you think and act. They will enhance your energy, positivity, mindset, and enthusiasm to reach out for your goals.

Let me make one thing clear at the onset: this is not a get rich quick book. That mentality doesn't work if you are looking for long-term wealth and success. The microwave mentality may make you rich for a while but I can place my last cent on the fact that it won't give you long-term and consistent wealth. The latter takes effort and discipline. It takes sweat, time, and work. You can't work 2 hours a week and expect to become a millionaire in a month.

Don't work on get rich quick schemes; instead channelize your energy towards get rich sure businesses and principles that will give you income in the long run. Ask any wealthy and successful person if they built their wealth in a few days, whether the transformation from nothing to everything happened overnight or a week or even a month! True wealth creation and success is a result of perseverance, discipline, consistent efforts, and resourcefully channelized efforts.

You have to keep building up efforts to rich the pinnacle of desired success, one building block at a time. Once you witness encouraging results or even tiny results or sometimes no results at, keep working at it. It may require a change in strategy or mindset. You may have to maneuver your direction slightly. At times, you may have to change the game plan completely. However, the important thing is to sustain, to keep going. That is the one major identifiable difference between successful and not so successful people.

What is stopping you from accomplishing your true success, glory, and destiny? Your parents? Spouse? Children? Bosses from hell? Co-workers? Nope, it is you. Your habits to be precise! You alone are stopping your success. Your mindset, actions, habits and mental chatter is the biggest obstacle to your own success. Stop blaming other people and circumstances for your situation, and start taking more ownership of your life. Each of is capable of accomplishing what we set our heart on if we have the power to believe in those dreams and chase them to reality with the help of constructive and positive habits.

9

Chapter 1: How Our Habits Define Us

i

There was once a great king who had heard about a master sword crafter who was said to be on par with Picasso when it came to his genius. The king decided he must meet this master sword crafter at once. He summoned his guards to find the sword crafter and bring him to the palace. The king's guards ran in all directions, looking for the maestro sword crafter, and finally found him in a tiny village on the outskirts of the kingdom. As ordered, they brought him before the king.

The master walked with him humbly, graciously and gently, and the king responded in a similar manner. The king then posed him a question he would ask all maestros. "Oh sword crafter, what is true secret to your extraordinariness or excellence in what you do?" Pat came the reply from the sword crafter, "Ever since I was a child, I became exposed to the art of making swords and fell madly in love with it. It seldom spoke to my brain, head, or logic; instead it spoke to me at a much deeper level and soulful level. It tugged at my heart. As a child I made a decision that I will be a master at sword crafting. Growing up, I read plenty of books about sword crafting. If a thing didn't relate to sword crafting, didn't have the word sword in it, didn't look like a sword, or had nothing to do with sword crafting, I wouldn't spend my time on it. That is the true secret of my mastery."

Let this powerful parable sink in your head for a while because in many ways; this is the secret to being exceptional, extraordinary, and world class! We function in a world inundated with distractions and fruitless pursuits. We are constantly pulled in different directions, and operate on auto-pilot, mindlessly going about things. This makes us time and productivity starved! Focus on few things that are important.

Let begin with a small and exciting exercise. What are the five most important things in your life? Maybe career/business, family, personal development, art, travel, whatever. Just pick five things that are most important and hold maximum value/relevance in your life. Now passionately build your life around it. Focus your time, energy efforts and much more on these all-important five things.

Clear all the other clutter and noise surrounding you that doesn't relate to or align with these five swords. This is in essence the secret to being productive. There are plenty of people who get bored and spend their most productive hours playing aggressive games, browsing through Instagram and checking their Facebook for the nth time.

They'll convince you they are being productive because they always look preoccupied. Looking busy doesn't necessarily mean they are being productive. What are you busy doing is the key? Are you doing something that is adding value to your overall goals? Are you busy doing things that are in alignment with your five swords? People won't distance themselves from what they are doing or step back and take an objective look at whether they are indeed involved in productive acts that are in alignment with their overall goals. They are in effect giving their best hours of their best days to nothing more than shiny objects.

Each time you find yourself digressing from your goals, think of the sword crafters metaphor. Dedicate yourself to the five things that matter most in your life (and let one of those five things not be Netflix or Playstation). Be among the 1 percent that focuses on things which really matter. Pull the courage to say no to activities and people who call for your time to make you unproductive. Have the fortitude to say no to activities that appear desirable or shiny but are plain hollow or have no value. This is the pathway to success, wealth and life mastery. True leaders aren't just ones with fancy titles. True leaders are those who inspire others with their work, self-discipline, and productivity.

Let's do another interesting and enjoyable exercise. Ready? Grab a notepad and paper and write down the names of 10 people on this planet you admire the most. Yes, 10 people whose life you really admire and seek inspiration from! It can be your favorite sports star, an entrepreneur, a technical wizard, an inventor, a movie star—just about anyone you truly, deeply admire. Take your time and think hard.

Done writing? Now, look for a common trait in all these people (other than the fact that they are all your idols of course). What is that one single trait which makes them all admirably successful? My bets are on self-discipline!

There is no long term success with self-discipline, which drives a person's ability to be productive and action-oriented. The people you admire are all hustlers. They keep getting things done, explore newer horizons, and follow effective habits to reach their goals. Self-discipline distinguishes the average from the extraordinary.

Notice how there is always a split second difference between athletes in crucial races. However, despite winning by a split second margin the winner takes it all while the athlete in second place has to contend with much lesser rewards. Though the difference was only in split seconds, the awards for winners are much greater. This split second difference is self-discipline. The ability to get yourself to do things! The ability to be productive and hustle your way to success, money, and mastery! The ability to go from ordinary to exceptional!

Unfortunately, there's no magic wand or potion for success and mastery. Much as I'd love you to be successful immediately, it's a gradual process. Attaining success is more like cooking in a crockpot than microwave. The microwave mentality of quick success and quicker failure doesn't last. Success has to brew for long if you want its flavor to sustain. You don't just have to adopt a successful mindset but also habits of successful masters who stand as testimony for the fact that building wealth, success, and life mastery need a conscious cultivation of self-discipline and powerful success habits. Are you geared for success? Much of it will be determined by tracking your daily habits and self-discipline patterns?

I remember having an interesting conversation with a friend once, where he mentioned that a majority of successful people just happen to be at the right place at the right time. They get plain lucky. Yes, I'd say being lucky can get you that one shot at success. However, without self-discipline and these 20 powerful habits that I am going to discuss, the success won't last.

Successful people display amazing time management skills, accept accountability for their actions, operate with a solution-oriented mindset, and have the tenacity to transform challenges into opportunities. They demonstrate great restraint, self-control, and the ability to delay greater while firmly fixating their eyes on the bigger picture or goals. Their habits define their success.

People with a success, wealth, and mastery mindset almost always have their actions driven by keeping their eyes firmly on long term rewards. This is the one trait that separates winners from strugglers. They are able to delay gratification or give up short term pleasures in exchange for long term rewards. Whether you are going to be a struggler or winner is in your hands? You alone are responsible for the choices you make!

There is no denying the element of luck and good fortune in writing a person's success. However, this success is also a direct result of meticulously cultivated and nurtured habits, actions, mindset, beliefs, and thoughts. We are nothing but an aggregation of our habits, thoughts, beliefs, and actions. Self-discipline and success habits (I like to call them success habits) are the ultimate bridge to achieving your goals.

Were you aware that 40 percent of all our behavior is determined by habits? If you are wondering why you aren't as successful as you desire, start by taking stock of your habits.

The people whose lifestyle, money, success, and fame you most likely admire are the ones who are awake at 5 am, run a few miles, meditate, have a fresh juice for breakfast, set tasks for the day—basically get things done. You'll seldom find them surfing aimlessly on the web, binge-watching Netflix, or refreshing their social media feed endlessly. They are constantly at work, either actually working or learning about ways to be more effective at work.

Every minute of their waking time is devoted towards being productive. They are feverishly working towards their destiny, building one block at a time.

Tell me something. Are you satisfied with where you are currently in your life? Have you truly achieved the success and glory you deserve? Are you living your dreams or simply existing on auto-pilot? If not, it's time for some major reprogramming and changes in everyday habits. You'll be stunned by how much can be accomplished by making tiny, gradual changes in your everyday habits, thought patterns, and mindset.

I am not talking some self-help humbug that looks good only on paper. I am talking real, actionable, practical, doable steps that can help you scale unimaginable heights. These are habits people have used to transform their life 360 degrees. By adopting these power-packed 20 habits, you will unlock the key to your true success and glory. You will unleash your fullest potential to lead a successful, wealthy, and glorious life.

These habits are designed to streamline efforts, instill more discipline in your life, and help you accomplish their success you deserve. They are proven to boost your energy, productivity, passion and enthusiasm towards your goals.

Are you still stuck with making a fast buck using one of the tons of crappy get rich quick schemes out there? Let me burst the bubble. It doesn't work! Build get rich sure careers and businesses that will help you build long-term wealth, which will take time, patience, consistent efforts and endless reserves of perseverance. True success and wealth creation need channelization of your energy towards businesses that last.

The transformation from nothing to everything is a result of self-discipline, efforts, and consciously channelized efforts. Once you begin to witness even tiny results, you'll be motivated to keep going. Success and results (however small) are the biggest drivers for even more success, wealth and results.

Building self-discipline is like building a muscle. The more you keep training it, the stronger and more formidable you become. The less you train and nurture it, the weaker and less effective you become. We all have muscular strength. Similarly, all of us possess self-discipline. Much like each person's muscular strength varies; people possess different degrees of self-discipline. Though everyone has it, not everyone has developed it. It takes muscle to create and grow more muscle. Similarly, it takes self-discipline to grow greater self-discipline. Have you used progressive weight training technique to build muscle? It is about lifting weights gradually until you can no longer lift anything more. You push your body's muscles until they give in, and finally, rest. There's always scope for more.

This is similar to how self-discipline works. You build discipline by dealing with challenges that can be successfully achieved but they are still near the limit. This doesn't translate into trying and failing each day at something new. It also doesn't imply staying in your cushy comfort zone. You don't gain strength by attempting to lift weight that cannot be budged nor do you gain strength by lifting weights that are increasingly light. You begin with weights/challenges that are within your current ability but they are also near your optimal limit.

In Progressive training, you keep increasing the challenge. If you stay within your comfort zone and keep working with the same weights capacity, you aren't getting any stronger buddy. Likewise, if you don't put yourself to test in life periodically, you don't gain self-discipline. Like a majority of people don't develop their muscles to their fullest potential with proper training, most people do not boast of high discipline levels.

Avoid pushing yourself too much when it comes to building self-discipline. That's not the best way to go about it. You can't transform your life 360 degrees in a day. It isn't realistic to go from slack king/queen to productivity ninja overnight. You can't set three dozen goals, and expect yourself to meet each of them consistently from the next day. It's a recipe for disaster. It is similar to a person hitting the gym for the first time and aiming to pack 300 pounds. It doesn't work and makes you look foolish!

If you can start with 15 pounds, so be it. There's nothing to hide or be ashamed of. You begin now and from where you currently are. No matter where you are with your discipline (even highly undisciplined), start. Begin with little self-discipline to build even more discipline. As you get stronger with discipline, the weights or challenges will seem much lighter.

Avoid comparing yourself with others. It will never work. Your expectations will be even harder to meet. If you believe you aren't strong, everyone will appear much stronger. Just look at where you currently are and aim to improve as you move ahead.

Lets us look at an example to understand this better. Assume you want to be able to put in 9 solid hours of productivity at work every day because you are aware that this will make a positive impact on your career. Plenty of our office time is spent socializing and indulging in unproductive vices. So obviously, there is plenty of scope for improvement where your goal is concerned.

To begin with, you start working for 9 hours with distractions and can manage to accomplish this only once. You are a disaster the next day. You can do one round of 9 hours for a day but not more. So let's cut back now. What duration will be able to sustain successfully for going an entire week? How about working with complete focus for an hour a day, five days in a row? Doable? If not, how about half an hour a day, five days in a row? Start with whatever you are comfortable with. If you think it's too easy a task, increase the challenge. The idea is to make it a mix of challenging and doable. Something that is a easy enough to be practical and challenging enough to inspire you.

Once you've work uninterrupted for an hour for a week, take it to next level during the subsequent week. Continue to persevere with the progression until you reach your goal of 9 productive hours each day. You are raising the bar gradually each week instead of doing it all at once, which doesn't sustain in the long run. Stay within your capability while also growing stronger. Once you build self-discipline, you slowly enjoy the benefits of everything you've done in the long haul. The training indeed produced value that makes your life more fulfilled, rewarding and gratifying. There are plenty of ways to build your self-discipline muscle, which you can get started with right away.

Chapter 2: Proven Ways to Develop and Sustain Powerful Habits

Do you know how Benjamin Franklin went about overcoming his negative habits and substituting them with more positive habits? He made a list of 13 virtues that were integral to his personal and professional life. The world famous leader then went about focusing on a single virtue for a week through a 13-week phase.

At the end of every week, he conquered the negative habit and then moved on to overcoming the subsequent habit.

Good habits are the foundation of self-discipline. When you develop good, positive, and constructive habits, it is easy to lead a controlled and disciplined life that spells success.

Wouldn't it be amazing if our life ran on auto-pilot? How about running, eating healthy, finishing projects on time, and more on auto-pilot? Unfortunately, that is not the way it works. You are pretty much in control of what you do. However, it becomes easier when you program your actions as constructive and positive habits. With little initial discipline, you can develop solid, life-long habits that can transform your personal and professional life. The real challenge is not to develop positive habits but to stick to them over the long haul.

Here are some of the most effective hacks to make and sustain positive habits.

Reward Yourself in Healthy Ways

The reason a lot of people develop bad or negative habits is because it gives them some of good feeling. If you take away this gratification or good feeling all at once, it will be challenging to sustain the good habit. Rather, get into the habit of rewarding yourself every once a while when you successfully manage to resist a temptation. For instance, if you manage to skip eating desserts throughout the week, reward yourself with a small pastry or cupcake on Sunday.

Similarly, treat yourself to your favorite café on a weekend if you manage to stay away from alcohol throughout the week. We seek a feel-good experience because it makes us feel less stressed. However, post the feel-good experience, we develop a feeling of guilt or regret. To prevent slipping into the old pattern of bad habits, give yourself an occasional reward. Ensure your rewards are healthy and balanced.

Buy yourself a new book, reward yourself with a new dress, watch a concert you've wanted to catch for long, purchase new exercise equipment and more. Even something as simple as a cup of your favorite latter or taking time out to visit an art gallery can be awesome rewards! You worked hard to earn these rewards and enjoy them guilt-free.

One of the best ways to give up unhealthy habits is to enlist the support of family and friends. Always inform people you trust about what you strive to achieve. They will show more understanding when you pass the drink or don't visit the pub with them post work or skip the dessert. In fact, they will motivate and support you to resist from the urge of slipping back into the old pattern. They will help you stay away from temptations, be your cheerleaders, and even lend the much required moral support when you are feeling down. We could all do with some cheerleaders who support us in accomplishing our goals.

One thing that works wonders for some people is to make yourself accountable to a few set of trusted people. For instance, you can give these people within your inner circle some money and ask them not to return it to you until you have implemented the good habit or resisted the urge to give in to the bad habit a specific numbers of times. For example, if you intend to lead a fitter life and give up junk food, ask a friend to return your money only after you have avoided junk food and eaten healthy for a week. This way you make yourself accountable to someone while developing positive habits.

Start Small and Give Yourself 30 Days

Again you can't start making big changes in your life suddenly. Habits need time to build and develop. Much as you are unhappy with your present happy, you can't transform it within a day. Many people are gung-ho about making too many sudden changes in their life, only to get overwhelmed and give up. For example, if you have made it your mission to devote 2 hours of your day to studying, don't start with two hours immediately.

Start slowly and gradually build on it. You can begin by studying for 30 minutes every day and slowly increase your study time. Instead of doing 100 push-ups a day, start with 10. Habits are likelier to be successful when you start small and gradually scale it up.

Notice and enjoy the small benefits of making these changes in your life. For example, if you've decided to lead a fitter or active life or lose weight, notice how you feel after a few minutes of exercise during the first few days. Did you notice any change in the energy level after beginning an exercise routine or a new diet? Visualize yourself getting higher grades and your dream job after changing your study habits.

According to research, it takes about four weeks for a habit to become automatic. If a person can sustain the initial mind conditioning cycle, the habit will become almost involuntary, and much more effortless to sustain. One month is a fairly decent time to commit to a positive habit. Much like Benjamin Franklin, block a month to develop and sustain a new habit.

Consistency is integral to the success of developing and sustaining new habits. If you have decided to run for a couple of kilometers each morning, get up and do it every day for the initial thirty days without any interruption. If you decide to go only on some days of the week, the habit will harder to sustain. Habits that are practiced in breaks are rather to lock in.

Do something continuously and without a break if you want to make it a habit. The more consistent and regular you are while following a habit, the easier and more effortless it becomes to stick to it.

Anticipate Potential Problems and Have a Plan to Tackle It

When you seek to develop positive habits or give up destructive habits, there will be some obstacles or challenges along the way. Plan your action steps in advance to combat these potential challenges.

Take for instance, you decide to go to the gym before heading to work by waking up at 6 every morning. There may be several challenges to this, including hitting the snooze when the alarm goes off at 6 am. Now, you are already aware of these potential challenges because you know you are not an early riser or may have unsuccessfully tried to wake up at 6 am each morning earlier.

However, now that you know the earlier approach hasn't worked, try to think of a new strategy where you are not setting yourself for another disappointment. Try of think of different ways, where more effort is needed to switch off the alarm clock. This will make it tough for you to go back to sleep. How about you setting the alarm a little further from the bed so you are forced to wake up and walk some distance to turn it off?

This way you much less likely to go back to bed since it has taken some effort to walk and you are now already wide awake.

Learn to reframe mistakes if your initial attempt isn't successful. Don't give up if your first try bombs. Give it another shot. Try to reframe these mistakes into solid opportunities. For all you know, trying a few times more may help you develop a positive habit or give up a negative habit. Researchers discovered that our brain has two possible responses to a mistake—solving the problem or shutting off from it.

When you consciously pay attention to the blunder, you can come up with novel ways to fight it and correct it in future. Shutting off from the mistake neurologically may feel good in the present moment. However, it doesn't help you in future circumstances. Observe closely where you lack or the mistakes you make so you are better able to tackle it in future.

Habits are continuous loops that we work on a more automated level. Have a clear if-then plan in place to break from the vicious loop of a bad habit and replace it with more positive habits. I know people who make flowcharts to guide them when potential challenges arrive or even when they successfully manage to resist the habit (reward time).

Swish

Swish is a Neuro Linguist Programming technique that has to do with training your mind through negative visualization. In the swish technique, a person visualizes himself/herself performing the negative habit. Next, imagine yourself eliminating the bad habit and replacing it with a more positive alternative.

Let's say you want to give up smoking. Visualize yourself physically lifting a cigarette and placing it down. Next, imagine/visualize yourself breathing fresh air or running away from the cigarette. Repeat this for a few times until you involuntarily experience the pattern before you actually give up the negative habit.

Make this power-packed tip even more impactful by combining it with a role model. Spend time with a person or people whose habits you want to model your own habits on. Recent research has discovered that people who had obese friends had higher chances of becoming fat. Thus, you truly become what you choose to spend your time and energy on.

Restructure your environment in a manner that makes it easy for you to give up the bad habit or form new, positive habits. For instance, if you want to give up alcohol, avoid taking a route that has too many bars on the way. Take a different route from work back home. Similarly, eliminate junk food from the house if you want to lead a fitter and healthier life. If you find yourself spending too much time on Netflix, cancel your subscription. Get rid of cigarettes and alcohol if you wish to give up addiction. Also, stop moving around in social circles that reinforce habits you wish to give up.

For example, if you plan to give up drinking, it is best to stop moving around or socializing with people who drink. This will eliminate your willpower struggle. Rather, find a buddy who will keep you upbeat and motivated about sticking to your habit.

Similarly, if you are keen to go to the gymnasium each morning before heading for work, keep your gym gear ready the previous night. Keep your gym bag all packed and ready at the entrance of the room. When you wake up in the morning, the first thing you'll see while stepping out of the room is the bag. This will remind you of your goal or habit to visit the gym each morning. These are environment clues that will help create the right setting for you to chase your positive habits and goals.

Use Positive Self-Talk

Bad habits made their way into your life for some reason. It could be low self-esteem, stress, lack of guidance, feeling of pleasure, or plain boredom. You could be biting your nails out of stress or drinking heavily due to sheer boredom. However, there's nothing that can't train your mind to do when you indulge in positive, encouraging, and inspiring self-talk. Bad or negative habits can be substituted with positive ones when you are honest with yourself and serious about making positive changes in your life through self-discipline.

There may be plenty of negative self-talk during the phase of overcoming bad habits. At times, you may not be successful in resisting an urge and may judge yourself harshly for being unable to control the habit. Show yourself some love and compassion. Don't keep reminding yourself how much you suck by indulging in negative self-talk.

Try to get into the habit of using "but" in your sentences each time you find yourself tempted to succumb to negative self-talk. Irrespective of what you say always add a "but" to your statement to transform it into a more constructive self-talk. For example, I may not be in perfect shape now but I could very well be in the next few months if I stick to my diet or "I am a failure at working on this project but I am learning new things and can get better at it each day if I spend less time playing games or watching television."

Each time you miss a workout, eat unhealthy food or sleep extra hours, you don't become a bad person. It isn't reason to slip back into the old pattern. A lot of people screw up a couple of times, and think they can't give up on a bad habit. That isn't true. You are not being a bad human; you're just being human.

Rather than whacking yourself hard for all the mistakes, plan for possible challenges in advance and keep pepping yourself through positive self-talk. Top performers aren't those who never go off track. They simply get back on track quicker than the others!

Keep your self-talk focused on the present rather than lacing it with anxiety of the future. When you feel caught in a habit or situation, think about how you can change it in the present, and let your self-talk revolve around it.

Chapter 3: Killing the Fear of Failure

Do you have an innate fear of failure that is stopping you from going after your dreams? Or maybe you've faced a few roadblocks and disillusionment and decided to give up your goal mid-way! Well let me tell you this straight and clear, most successful people you look up to and admire haven't had it any easier than you (even if you believe otherwise). No, they haven't! They've only stuck around and readjusted their sails in the middle of the windy sea instead of throwing up the sails and resigning to their fate.

When it comes to limiting or enhancing your chances of success, the most important factor is your perception. By altering your perception, you can program your mind for greater success. The good news is that it isn't tough to create a breakthrough mindset that perceives setbacks as opportunities and learning and not obstacles. You can easily work through barriers that place limitations on your and develop strategies for countering these so-called obstacles that come in the way of your success and abundance.

There is a Buddhist story about king whose kingdom was filled with self-entitled citizens. Not happy with this, he decided to teach them a lesson they wouldn't forget. He had a simple and ingenious plan. He placed a massive boulder right in the center of the main street, blocking people's entry. The king decided to hide in the bushes nearby and observe his citizens' reactions.

He wondered how they would react. Would they get together and discard it? Would they feel disillusioned and returned? The king watched with disappointment as one subject after another gave up and returned rather than attempting to remove the boulder from their path. At best, some tried to lift it half-heartedly but quickly gave up. Many people openly uttered expletives towards the king or grumbled about the inconvenience without thinking of ways to move past it.

After a few days, a peasant happened to come across the boulder. Instead of turning back like the others, he tried to push the boulder out of his way several times. Then suddenly, an idea struck him. He went to the adjoining woods to look for a large branch that he used as a lever dislodge the huge rock from the street. As soon as the massive rock moved, beneath it was a bag of good coins and a handwritten note from the king stating, "The obstacle in the path becomes the path. Never forget, within every obstacle is an opportunity to improve our condition."

Are you using the obstacles in your path to your advantage? Are you leveraging the power of the challenges in your life to convert them into opportunities? Like we discussed earlier, obstacles are opportunities in disguise. Do you have the foresight to covert disillusionments in your life into wealth and success? Here are a few strategies for changing your perception towards challenges and using it to build greater wealth and success.

One of the biggest differences between people who witness massive success in life and those that struggle to make a living is that the former do not give up on their goals even when the going gets tough. They truly believe in the power of their dreams and in their ability to make those dreams come true.

Do you know the story of J.K Rowling, one of the richest people in the United Kingdom and one of the wealthiest authors in the world? It took her years of perseverance and dedication to her goal to take her there.

Rowling hit upon the idea of creating a fictional character by the name of Harry Potter. No sooner did she hit upon this idea, Rowling had to deal with the death of her mother. She stopped writing the book and dived deep into grief and depression— pretty much where none of us ever want to be. She got virtually nothing accomplished during this phase.

In an effort to pull herself out of the throes of depression, Rowling began to teach English language in Portugal. She made it her goal to finish writing her first Harry Potter novel by the time she moved out of Portugal. The idea of moving was to help herself get away from the grief and stress.

Of course, things don't always go as per our plan. She didn't make any progress with her book and to add to her woes, she ended up with a failed marriage and a little daughter to look after. Back to square one, she had nothing left. There was no job, no book to publish, and her daughter to feed with measly unemployment benefits. She didn't have the means to keep her home warm, owing to which Rowling made frequent trips to the local cafe. This was her only way of keeping her little baby warm and comfortable. She resumed writing while the little one slept in the cafe.

When she finished drafting a few chapters, she sent the manuscript to one publisher after another who kept rejecting it under the pretext that it didn't look promising enough to entice readers. Her mailbox began filling up with rejection letters. She had 12 different publishers reject her manuscript.

What would you have done in a similar scenario? Thought that 12 different publishers can't be wrong and that maybe you are really not good at this and should try doing something else instead, right? This wasn't her attitude or thought process though. Rowling believed in what she had created. She truly believed in the power of her goals and dreams.

The editor of Bloomsbury Publishing sat down with his eight-year-old daughter to read Rowling's manuscript. The little girl loved it and wanted to read the entire book. This made the publisher agree to the proposal of getting Rowling's book published. However, she was also told to get a steady full-time job since writing children's fantasy books could never be a career option. Aren't we all secretly chuckling knowing what she's worth now and the fortune she's earned from this series?

The Harry Potter series has been translated into over 70 languages across the world and sold millions of copies. Not just that, it has acquired $20 billion via movie rights and sponsorships alone. And this author began to draft her series as a single poor, divorced, and depressed mother.

Imagine if like a majority of us, she'd given up midway after a few rejections and not believed in the power of her goals and dreams. In most likelihood, she would've still been the struggling single mother trying to make ends meet rather than one of the world's richest people. There is huge lesson in this story for each one us. The power of perseverance and overcoming challenges by keeping your eyes firmly on your goal.

Yes, there are no excuses for failure! No one except yourself and your self-limiting mindset holds you back. What is your definition of failure? Do you let it get the better of you by giving up? In this case it is your enemy! Or do you learn the right lessons and convert it into a brilliant opportunity? If yes, failure becomes your ally, doesn't it? Are you bogged down by failure or do you have the courage to get up, brush off the dust, and give it a good fight all over again? Like I mentioned earlier, failure as either be a stumbling block or stepping stone. It is your perception to failure that defines your success! Fear of failing is worse than failure itself because it confines you to a life of untapped potential.

No person is perfect. Even the rich and famous people you admire have gone through their share of trials and tribulations to emerge victorious. They've failed too. And many more times than you've even tried! Thomas Edison tried to create the light bulb unsuccessfully in a thousand different ways. Have you even tried something 1,000 times? And you wonder why you are not the next Edison, Zuckerberg, or Steve Jobs! The difference is these people have the conviction to convert their challenges and failures into triumphs, something which most people don't do.

That is why there are only so many super successful people. It's the attitude!

Did you know Oprah Winfrey was sacked as the news anchor of a Baltimore channel for becoming too emotionally invested in the news stories? Her characteristic trait that went on to define Oprah's diva anchor status and made her one of the highest paid television personalities of all times! Henry Ford's financers pulled out a couple of times before he produced a passable automobile prototype. The list of successful people who've turned failure on its head is endless. If you want to be one among them, here are some ways clever people utilize failure to their advantage.

1. Acknowledge your mistakes. It takes courage to admit that you screwed up and that is the first step towards success. Own up your mistakes and accept responsibility for your actions rather than blaming other people or external circumstances. When you take responsibility for your actions, you are in control of your life. When you acknowledge your mistake, you hit upon the realization that this isn't the best way to do it. The first step towards changing any habit, behavior pattern, action, thought process, and strategy is to acknowledge that there is a problem.

Once you identify the problem, acting upon it becomes easier. For instance, if you realize or own up that you are not able to save much because of irresponsible spending habits, you'll take measures to work upon it. Identifying the root cause and acknowledging your failures sets the momentum for future transformation in a positive direction.

2. Keep the right perspective. I'll tell you a little story here that was published in the *Chicken Soup for the Soul series*. There was a pair of identical twins. While one child was a beaming optimist, the other was a cynical and hopeless pessimist. Their parents were predictably worried about this and brought them to the neighborhood psychologist. To balance their thought process and personalities, the psychologist suggested a small yet significant exercise. On their birthday, both were assigned separate rooms to pick up their gifts.

The pessimist entered his room to see it filled with the best toys their parents could buy. There were games, a computer, a toy car, a calculator—pretty much everything a child would want. The optimist, on the other hand, entered a room full of manure. The parents carefully hid in the corridor to note the results on the exercise on the boys' thinking. The pessimist twin complained about the color of the computer and the material out of which the calculator was made. He thought the game wasn't good enough for him and that his friend had a bigger car than the one he'd been given.

In the other room, the optimist was jumping with joy. He was delightfully flinging the manure up in the air saying, "You can't really fool me! Where there is this much manure, there's gotta be a pony!" See the difference? It's your perspective that matters. Do you see it as a monster that is out to stop your success and abundance? Or is an angel in disguise that is leading to the right direction by telling you what not to do now? You can either view failure as a stumbling block or stepping stone. The choice is yours! And the perspective with which you view failure will largely determine your chances of success.

Remember you can't always choose your circumstances and things that happen to you in life. However, you can choose your reaction to it. You can't always determine the course your life may take but you can choose your perception and response to it. Winners see opportunities, losers see excuses. Control how you perceive and approach an obstacle. This can be done by control your catastrophic thinking or irrational emotions. Don't think in terms of extremes. One failure or lay off doesn't spell doom for your career. One bad business deal doesn't mean it is time to shut shop. Avoid blowing things out of proportion and see them in a more balanced light. See things as they are and not what you think they are. You are reorienting your mind or selectively editing your thoughts to develop a victory mindset even in the midst of so-called failure. The right perspective can lead to positive actions.

3. Stay persistent. Few things are more responsible for your success than the ability to stay afloat despite being in choppy waters. You can't cross the ocean by looking at it from the shore. You have to go there, face the grind, fail, and then get up again to succeed. There will be people who will make you give up on your dreams and saying it's impossible. Who knew Walt Disney could create a world like Disneyland?

People laughed at Galileo when he stated the earth moves around the sun. Popular perception around that time was that the sun moved around the earth, which was believed to the epicenter of the universe. When people say something can't be done, remember they are referring to their inability to do it, which doesn't necessarily define yours! Persistence is nothing but optimism at work.

When regular people say that's enough and quit, winners say I am not doing enough and continue. Instead of quitting, they take on challenges with gusto and stay persistent. Despite witnessing setbacks, they stay consistent in their wealth and success building efforts. Like the proverbial phoenix, they are unafraid of rising from the ashes.

4. Your "Why" keeps you going. Well, your why will keep you going even when the "how" becomes difficult. When you have a clear why in place, the how can be figured out. If you know you are doing something to give your children the best life possible, you will keep going with this purpose in mind even when things get tough. You won't be tempted to give up because that means giving up on a strong purpose in your life. It is easier to throw in the towel when you don't have a compelling reason for doing something. A strong reason will keep you motivated and afloat even in the stormy sea.

Sometimes when you are stuck in the middle of a seemingly impossible situation, the best thing to do is think! You create plenty of opportunities and avenues by thinking rationally and objectively. Create movement by thinking things such as how can I solve this problem or challenge? If I can't solve it, how can I make it better for myself and other people? You'll be surprised by how a few simple and positive questions can change the way you approach the issue at hand. Think about other people, especially your loved ones.

This gives you the strength to overcome challenges. The next time you are feel overwhelmed by a challenge, don't sit there and curse your fate. If you don't try, you will not go far from where you are currently and you'll never grow. All the people you admire have at some point or the other faced and overcome obstacles, which is responsible for their current glory. Instead of suffering their less then desirable circumstances, they made the most of the challenges presented to them. If your bigger picture is to retire by the time you are 40 or earn financial freedom for your family or any other compelling reasons, you'll keep going despite obstacles.

5. Imperfect action is better than no action at all. Plenty of times, people try to swim by trying to judge the depth of the water from the shore. What if I fail? Really now, the amount of success stories we've missed because people didn't tap into their real potential

owing to the fear of failure. Remember, taking action is better than not doing anything. Failing is a million times better than not trying. It gives you insights that inaction won't! Even if you fail, you know a different way to do something that will take you a step closer to success and wealth creation.

Let's say you start a social media page and post great content (at least you think you do). You promote it aggressively to reach the right audience. However, you don't receive a lot of engagement or comments on your post. Now, you know you aren't doing something right. The problem is either the followers you are targeting are not a right fit for the page or your posts are not appealing enough for them, which means you need to change your content strategy. How would you know this if you hadn't created the page in the first place out of fear of not generating enough followers? Now you have insights about what isn't working. Equipped with this knowledge, you can change your strategy and set things right. You'll never try if you are afraid of failure and you'll never learn if you don't try!

6. Turn the monster on its head. There is plenty of positives in everything if we only have the vision to look for it. The things that we believe to be negative can hold plenty of positives. A

technical glitch that you think has destroyed all your work is a chance of you to work on it again and make it even better than the previous one because now you are more prepared and knowledgeable. Remember, the friend who lost his job and went on to set up his own profitable venture? What if he wouldn't have been laid off by his organization? He'd still be a bucket carrier, working round the clock to accomplish someone else's profits rather than building wealth for himself.

Having a boss who is negative and discouraging is a wonderful opportunity to learn what you shouldn't be as a boss or brush up your resume for a better job in another organization. Trust me, every situation will have some good in it. You just have to be perceptive enough to spot it.

7. Let go of challenges that are beyond your control. As much as you'd like to control everything in your life, some challenges are going to be beyond your control. Think devaluation of your home due to a natural calamity in the region or losing your job owing to a merger or global recession. These are circumstances where you have little control. Instead, focus on challenges that you can control. For example, not knowing a particular skill that can help you earn more money or grow your business is a challenge that

you can easily overcome by mastering it. If you haven't graduated yet, which is posing to be a challenge in your future job prospects or making more money, go and get that degree. Take away focus from challenges that can't be controlled and instead give attention to the ones that can be overcome.

8. Grow bigger than the challenge. While the poor mindset views their problem and often attribute it to bad luck or circumstances, the rich mindset will scratch their heads hard until they discover a solution. They'll seldom quit. Instead, they'll change the course of their action or try a different way to do it.

The rich, unlike the average Joes, don't have an either-or mentality. I can either purchase this or that. Instead, they will find a way to buy both by delaying gratification. They won't seek immediate pleasure but will work towards getting everything they want. Let us say a person with a wealthy mindset has $10. Now, they want both ice-cream and candy a $10. Instead of thinking, I can either have candy or ice-cream, they'll avoid buying both. They'll go ahead and buy a four dozen bottles of packaged water and sell it to thirsty travelers for 50 cents each to make a cool $24. Now they can buy candy, ice-cream and have a few dollars' spare. The wealthy hold a "both" not "either-or" mentality.

Chapter 4: Recognize Your Goal

Yes, you want to accomplish certain dreams and goals, which is why you are reading or hearing this book. However, do you know why you want it? For instance, I asked one of my clients why they wanted to launch a business. He stated in a very matter of fact manner that they wanted a big house, a fast car, and the best vacations money could buy. I repeated my question. Again, he said because he wanted all the material possessions he mentioned above. I asked him for the third time and he lost all patience by now and snapped at me. I calmly told him, he was only mentioning materials possessions or the means to an end, which were not really his end. Then, something struck him and he quickly realized his folly and said, "Because I want to give my family the best life possible."

What is your "why" that will drive you towards your goals with the right zeal, motivation and enthusiasm. When you define your "why" the "how" invariably chalks its path. You have to know why you want to accomplish something or what is the higher purpose or reason for accomplishing something before you can chase it with all you have. Your why keeps you on course in choppy waters. It will help you stay strong and motivated when the going gets tough. Each of us has a "why" that needs to be discovered and not everyone has the same "whys." Someone may work hard for the bigger purpose of giving their children a good life and education; others may work hard to travel around the world. Still others may work hard because it is their dream to open an art school. Each of us has a distinct why that drives us. Identifying your why is the first and most important step to achieving success, wealth and life mastery.

Defining your why at the outset is important because each time you are tempted to throw in the towel in the face of obstacles, your "why" will prevent you from doing it. When challenges knock you down, it will allow you to get up, shake the dust and continue your efforts. Your "why" will sustain you in the long run!

The "why" gives you a value-centric and purposeful life. Define your "why" clearly. Why do you want to do something—financial freedom, more time with family, travel around the world, give a good life to your loved ones, start an NGO, open a dance school, or are simply passionate about your goal! The why is integral to your success! Even when figuring out the how, the "why" plays a huge role. How badly do you want something is determined by your "why" and if your "why" is strong, you are unstoppable. Being a hustler and "goal digger" comes easy when your "why" is in place.

We've all played video games, right? They are a fantastic analogy for life itself. There are multiple levels, obstacles, and energy boosters/life givers! Hell, if I put aside a penny for the number of times I've got thrown off the course by the obstacles, I'd own a gold charter plane by now. We face monsters and enemies trying to throw us off guard. However, we don't give up playing. Your resolve to win deepens with every defeat and you play until you knock down those enemies and obstacles. Life isn't any different really!

If you have a powerful "why", you continue playing instead of quitting. If you have a powerful "why", you will not just try to pass classes but to ace them! With strong "why", you won't simply work to pay your bills but will make enough to travel around the world. You "why" will not just help you write a screenplay that gets made into a movie, you'll write an Oscar-winning screenplay. The difference between success/excellence and failure/mediocrity is often a "why." If you haven't already defined your "whys", do it now!

You can't calm every storm that comes in your way. However, you can calm yourself during the storm and the storm will eventually pass.

Knowing your "why" awards you the filter to wield choices and decisions about your personal and professional life to gain greater fulfillment in everything you do.

Irrespective of whether you are a businessman, an employee, a team leader, a freelancer, an intern, student or whoever, you want a clear why to inject passion into your work. Without purpose or passion, you be likelier to give up when the course gets rough. Those who operate with a solid "why" possess the ability to not just do great work but also inspire those around them. This is because people with a powerful "why" are very driven.

I'll let you in on one of the most unfortunate aspects of human existence. A majority of people live their life by accident. Things will happen to them by chance. We take things as they come, going with the flow, and living as life happens on auto-pilot mode. This is merely surviving or existing, not living. Living comes with fulfillment, which in turn is a result of purpose. When you derive a sense of fulfillment from your purpose, you keep going. You don't simply exist, you live. You don't act to survive; you act go conquer.

Today's work life isn't a cakewalk. You get up early. Drive to work. Deal with a pesky boss and at times even peskier co-workers. Then, you hustle to make money and spend sleepless nights trying to complete a deadline. Rinse. Repeat. There are plenty of challenges to deal with on a day to day basis.

The work world can be tough: Wake up, go to work, deal with the boss, make money, come home, manage your personal life, go to bed, wake up, repeat. That's plenty to deal with every day. Why get fancy by trying to also understand why you do what you do? Your "why" will prevent you from functioning on auto-pilot mode where things happen to you. Instead, with a clear purpose, you will make things happen.

When you identify your "why", you are able to seek greater clarity, discipline and confidence to make choices about your relationships, career, communities, and other institutions. You will aim to inspire and be inspired in everything you do.

Do you want to wake up each morning with an infectious energy, enthusiasm, and passion for work? Do you want to get home feeling fulfilled at the end of every single day? The secret is— WHY.

If you've faced a considerable crisis in life, you would've experienced the power of having a purpose. You'll tap into inexhaustible reserves of energy, courage, perseverance, and determination that you were not even aware you possessed.

When your mission is clear, you'll have laser-like focus. Think of the purpose as the light energy focused via a magnifying glass. When the light is diffused, it is useless. However, when the same light energy is concentrated via a magnifying glass, it can set the paper on fire. Focus it even more with a laser beam and the light energy can slice steel.

Similarly, a clear purpose lets you concentrate all your efforts on priorities, on things that matter the most. It will push you to take risks and move ahead, regardless of obstacles and setbacks.

What is the major difference between humans and animals? Humans, unlike animals, desire much more from their life than just survival. Without answering the question what are we surviving for? You'll be overcome by feelings of depression, despair, and disillusionment if you don't have a purpose!

Ever wondered why there is an alarming increase in the instances of substance abuse, suicide, and mental ailments like depression? Or why is there a growing dependence on anti-depressants? The likeliest reason is lack of purpose and true meaning.

You know you are doing something but you don't know why you are doing it. People are wealthier today than they've ever been, yet, unfortunately, there's a huge gap between well-placed and well-being. This is because wealth alone is pointless without a lack of purpose.

A new hire once went to the HR manager and stated that he wasn't keen to continue working in the organization. When questioned by the HR personnel, he stated that the workplace was filled with negativity where people talk badly about each other, engage in politics, and gossip.

The HR guy then told him that he could leave the organization if he fulfilled one task sincerely. He was to take a glass full of water and walk around the office thrice without spilling a single drop. After completing the task, the employee could leave, the HR stated.

The new recruit got to work immediately and walked thrice around the office without spilling a single drop on the floor. He went to the HR and told him he had successfully completed the task. The HR then questioned him about whether he heard other employees talk badly about each other, gossip, or create disturbances. He replied in the negative. The HR also asked him if anyone looked at him in a negative manner. The recruit again replied in the negative.

The HR then went on to tell the new recruit that he had a clear goal: to avoid spilling water, which was directly linked to his purpose of wanting to quit the organization. The same is true with our life. When we have a clear purpose, we focus on our priorities instead of other people's negatives or mistakes!

All the people I know realize that they've got to work really hard and many of them work hard! However, only a handful of them know what they truly want to accomplish from the hard work. How do plan to get anything in life if you don't even know what you want or what you are working for? Will you reach your destination if you don't enter an address in your GPS? Money isn't really a well-defined goal. How will you realize you've made sufficient money to fulfill your goal of making more money? How much is more? Does more money translate into a private jet, an expensive car, or vacations aboard every six months? Setting clear goals or whys awards you the gratification of knowing that your goals are fulfilled when you accomplish them. Let your whys be crystal clear and well-defined.

There is no pathway or thumb rule for identifying your "why." There are several ways through which you can gain greater insights about your life's purpose by knowing yourself and developing a larger understanding of how you can contribute to the world. What can you offer? What is your main value proposition? These and several other questions will help you discover your purpose. To help you find the sweet spot of your "why", here are some questions to ask yourself.

1. What are you inherent strengths?

In the book The Element, author Sir Ken Robinson aptly states that our true element is the sweet point at which our innate talent and skill merges with personal passion. When a person is in his/her true element, they become more productive, instill more value in the world, and enjoy greater personal as well as professional fulfillment. And surprise surprise—they make more money!

What are the things that you've been good at always? What are the things that come to you with ease and you often wonder why others find it so challenging? Are you naturally creative and innovative to come up with out of the box ideas? Are you a genius where details are concerned, naturally executing projects that need precision? Are you a gifted communicator who doesn't have any difficulty in articulating or expressing yourself clearly? Are you a diplomat, negotiator, leader, solution-provider, good listen, networker, change agent, technocrat? What are your natural strengths?

Now, you may or may not be passionate about what you possess a natural talent for. A fine, agile, and graceful dancer may not be passionate about dancing. Similarly, someone who has knack for writing really well may not be a passionate writer. However, a majority of people do not show aspirations and ambitions towards things they aren't good at. You are less likely to be passionate about programming when you don't possess an inherent aptitude for technology. Get the drift?

Howard Thurmon put it across brilliantly when he said, "Don't ask yourself what the world needs; ask yourself what makes you come alive, then do that. Because what the world needs is people who have come alive."

2. How do you measure life?

If you don't stand for something, you'll fall for just about anything! How do you want your life to be measured? Measuring your life means taking a clear stand for stand for something and then aligning your existence to it.

Living with a strong purpose is focusing on things that matter the most to you. Having said that, something that matters most to you will rarely be "things!" While some folks have the liberty of swapping the security of a regular 9-5 job to chase their passion, others have short term goals and responsibilities to take care of— they are thinking about paying off a debt, providing for their kids, paying bills, and more. However, you don't really have to choose between money and passion all the time. Sometimes, a plain shift in the perspective and ideas can change your experiences.

Identifying your purpose pushes you to accept challenges and stretch you beyond your comfort zone to inspire you. A boat under pressure can manage a wave of any magnitude if it is placed perpendicular to it. Similarly, your perspective and purpose can help you tackle any challenge.

3. What makes you alive?

This is one important question that will get you thinking in the right direction when it comes to identifying your purpose. What is it that makes you come alive? What are the things that inspire you? What is it that lights up a fire in your belly? When I say what makes you come alive, I am not referring to your video games or favorite football team games or your fancy wardrobe (unless you are sports professional or stylist), I am referring to a purpose that's something bigger. It is about connecting at a deeper level with what you are passionate about? It is the awareness that when you are passionate about something and put your attention on it, you can increase your influence and positive impact in ways that few other things can. It is taking on endeavors that light a fire in your belly to make a difference.

Of course, you don't have to be the big ticket inventor or find the cure for cancer (though why not?). This is about discovering a cause that is higher than you but is also in alignment with who you truly are as a person.

4. Where can you add the highest value?

Taking on something you are innately good at but hate doing is not the best route to fulfillment. However, knowing your inherent strengths and merging it with where you can add maximum value through the implementation of your knowledge, aptitude, education, skills, experience, and more helps you concentrate on professional opportunities and roles where you have high chances of succeeding while also awarding you a high sense of achievement, fulfillment and contribution.

People tend to undervalue the abilities and skills that they have a natural expertise for. Try to reframe the concept of value addition by asking yourself: "What problem can you help solve within your organization?" "What are the problems that you are passionate about solving or that give you a sense of fulfillment while solving?" This way, you'll focus more on your inherent strengths and the things you are naturally good at than trying to overcome your weaknesses.

5. If money wasn't an issue, what would you do?

This is a good question to ask yourself for determining if you are being driven by money alone or also have passion go along with it.

Money drives a good number of us. However, it may not always be the primary driver or purpose of your life. It can be just one of the many "whys" or a means to fulfill a "why." Your "why" may be to open a cancer treatment research institute or a charity which needs a good amount of money. Look at what you are currently doing and question yourself if you'd still do it if money was not a consideration. Would you? Be honest. If you had all the money in the world, would you still do what you are presently doing? There is a high chance that your answer is NO! If your answer is no (which means you are a part of the majority), you are stuck in a job! I won't say get up now and become a professional athlete, a ballet dancer, or a runway model – that's slightly unrealistic (though let no one define your parameters of realistic and unrealistic).

However, you need a career not a job you are stuck in. A rewarding, fulfilling career that you love and that drives you to get up each morning and head to work. When you are in a career you love, you'll give it your best shot, which will increase your chances of success and wealth. Again, if you are 9-5 bucket carrier, you can't quit everything overnight and run behind what you love doing. You'll begin with one step a time, climbing one rung after another to slowly make your way to the top. The "why" helps you wake up in the morning and give it your all. Unless you plug into your purpose and take action towards fulfilling that purpose, your chances of success are dim! When you plug into your "why", the how is never a challenge.

If you do something you are deeply passionate about, you boost your success chances. When you toil on something that lights up your fire, it stops seeming like work. It is similar to building a dream, one task at a time. Pick something that you have a huge interest in. Combine this with external rewards, a sense of inner fulfillment and value addition, and you'll find your "why." You'll pour everything into it if you are driven by a deep passion and desire to do something. All successful people from Bill Gates to Steve Jobs were visionaries and passionate about what they were doing.

If you do something merely for external rewards or money, it may not be sustained in the long run. Sustained efforts will be a challenge after the initially euphoria fades. You'll probably quit and find other ways to make money. However, if you are guided by passion, your drive to keep going in the face of obstacles will help you stay on course. This is because the passion will bring a sense of fulfillment!

Having said that let me also reiterate that passion alone doesn't survive for long if it doesn't generate the required results. You may be passionate about writing poems. However, if it doesn't help you sustain financially or help you lead a decent life, it'll wither faster than you realize. This is exactly why your purpose or why has to be the sweet spot between intrinsic and extrinsic motivators.

6. What past signposts can I use to define your future?

Go back to your past to discover the getaway to your future. It may help you define your purpose. What made you tick as a child when there were no worldly considerations? What were the things you loved doing or derived pure joy out of during your childhood and teen years? Did you derive great joy from playing a particular sport? Or participating in dramas/theatre? How about playing a musical instrument, writing poems or painting? Drawing comic characters, playing video games or looking after animals?

I know most of you will want to hit me hard now and say, "But we can't make money out of all these childhood passions when reality hits us?" Why not? Idea and a game plan are the key. I know many successful artists and painters who make a killing by auctioning their artworks. They employ slick marketing ideas and resourcefully tap into multiple channels to convert their passion into a financially rewarding profession. What stops a passionate horse rider from making a killing out of taking horse riding lessons for enthusiasts? What is stopping you from developing ideas into money-making opportunities? Your own inner, self-limiting beliefs! Passion and monetary rewards aren't mutually exclusive. You can have both. There are innumerable examples around you of people who love doing what they do, which in turn helps them make even more money. So next time, someone asks you or you ask yourself—passion or financial rewards—say both!

Go back to your past for references on how you can shape your future. What are the things that you loved doing when money was not a criterion? You'll find some truly revealing answers!

A man came across three laborers who were busy laying bricks. He questioned the first bricklayer about what he was up to. "Can't you see I am laying bricks on the plot?" The man then asked the second laborer what he was doing, "I am building a wall", he replied. Finally, the passerby went to the third bricklayer and similarly questioned him about what he was doing. Pat came the reply, "I am building a church here."

Did you notice the three distinct perspectives? All three men were doing the exact same work yet the way they viewed their work or the purpose with which they were doing it differed. While one saw it a merely laying bricks on the plot, the other's purpose was to build a church. The first worker most likely was the one who was only concerned about his paycheck. He viewed his work as a task that had to be completed only for money. The first laborer wasn't too concerned about the outcome. He was the first one to run out once the end bell rang. The second laborer was probably driven by the need to complete his task and derive a sense of fulfillment from the completion of his task. He is the type who would put in some extra time and effort to see task to its completion.

However, it was the third laborer who was driven by a desire to create a religious structure, which would bring divinity to the community and increase worship. There was a higher purpose to his work than simply getting his paycheck or completing the task. This higher purpose drove him to be the best in his job. Every brick that he laid was seen as a vision of grandiose, glory and aspiration. He was the type of worker who would do everything it takes to bring his vision to fulfillment.

Here are some questions you can ask yourself for figuring out your why if you haven't already found it by now.

1. Why do you do what you do?

2. What excites you about your present job or career?

3. What is your idea of a fantastic day?

4. What is success to you beyond your paycheck?

5. How does real success feel?

6. What do you desire to feel about your influence on the world once you retire?

7. What do you dislike about your present job or career?

8. Why aren't you doing something else?

9. What does a typical bad day look like?

10. What are the things you don't really enjoy about your work?

11. What is failure for you beyond the paycheck?

12. What does failure look like to you?

Other than knowing what you want, your purpose can also be defined by what you don't want. When you know what you don't want, you'll know what you are truly chasing, which helps define your purpose in life.

What are your intrinsic and extrinsic motivators?

Intrinsic motivation is behavior that is guided by internal rewards. In simple words, the motivation to do something originates from the individual because he/she feels an internally rewarded for it. There are three main types of intrinsic motivators according to Weinberg and Gould — knowledge, stimulation, and accomplishment.

A person may do something for a genuine thirst of acquiring knowledge or learn more about a subject. Similarly, a person can feel motivated to do something to enjoy a sense of accomplishment or achievement. Stimulation or challenging/interesting tasks that drive us to do our best are also a form of intrinsic motivation. The rewards come from within us not outside of us unlike extrinsic motivation.

Extrinsic motivation is behavior impacted by external rewards such as grades, fame, wealth, and applause/praise. This originates from outside the individual in contrast to intrinsic motivation, which comes from within. Performance related rewards can drive an individual to action. To stay on the course of your goals, you need a healthy combination of both intrinsic and extrinsic motivation. You should be internally driven by a purpose and external driven by the rewards that come from fulfilling the goal. An inner sense of fulfillment and external rewards both are integral to the purpose of goal fulfillment.

Make a list of your intrinsic and extrinsic motivators before you head any further. Remember, each person's definition of success is different because their "why" is different from yours. For someone, giving their family comfortable life can term them a success. For others, it can be the power and ability to touch other people's life selflessly that can be termed a success. Still, others may view going back to college and getting a degree as success. Your definition of success is a good indicator of your "why."

Talk to any life coach or self-help guru and they'll tell you how a majority of people sadly do not utilize their maximum potential. If you have to unlock your true potential and live the glorious life you are destined to live, connect with yourself at a deeper level to explore your passions.

If you are like several other people caught in the grind of their daily life, you may not have discovered your true passion or potential yet. This may be stopping you from accomplishing several life goals. Eliminate could have and would've have from your life and seize complete control of it by discovering your passion.

Here are some effective guidelines for helping you explore your true potential.

1. Explore multiple options to know what you are good at. Do different and new things by getting out of your comfort zone. Widen your social circle. Attend networking events, business conferences and seminars. Sometimes, if you are fortunate, your passion will strike you instinctively. You may be clicking photographs and you'll suddenly realize that this is something you love or enjoy doing. Keep exploring options, opportunities, and possibilities until you come across something you enjoy doing. Make excelling in that field your goal. We need to discover and explore our passion to come up with rewarding and gratifying goals.

2. Weed out the negativity surrounding you. It can drain your positive energy and stop you from accomplishing your goals. Surround yourself with positive, inspiring, encouraging, and goal-oriented people who push you to achieve your dreams. There are lots of energy vampires around us, who drain and positive energy and replace it with their negativity. They will tell

you something can't be done based on their own inability to do it not your potential. Some people are unable to discover their calling or don't possess the courage to chase their dreams, which makes them frustrated and discontent in life. This discontentment, frustration, and negativity is often passed on to others. Beware of such people and don't allow them the privilege of crushing your dreams or goals. Follow your passion with perseverance.

3. The environment plays a huge role when it comes to helping us discover or explore our passion. At times, if the place we grow up may not have presented us with the opportunities we seek in life. You may not have had the required resources or options to discover your passion. However, it's never too late to start identifying your passions for chalking out your goals.

4. Identify your values, strength, hobbies, and personalities to reach out to your true calling. What are your core values, beliefs, and ideals in life? How can you align your personal and professional goals with these values? Our passion generally originated from our strengths, personality, and beliefs. Our valued determine to a large extent the type of goals we chalk out.

Once you've identified a passion that aligns with your beliefs and values, work towards fulfilling it purposefully.

5. Silence your inner critic periodically. Sometimes, the negativity and criticism doesn't originate from outside. It comes from inside us. We are our biggest critics. Our self-limiting, negative, and destructive self-talk can kill our goals. For example, you may want to give up smoking. However, your monster of your critical self-talk make rear its ugly head and tell you it's impossible because you are completely hooked now. The fear, uncertainty, anxiety and lack of confidence can prevent you from successfully chasing your goal.

Start being more mindful and attentive to your self-talk. What are the things you are generally saying to yourself? Do you use more negative than positive words while talking to yourself? Do you encourage or crush your inner spirit while talking to yourself? If you are prone to negative self-talk, try converting into a more positive and constructive conversation with the self. Gently and slowly replace your negativity and insecurity with more positive and encouraging self-talk. For example, instead of saying I cannot do something or I am not good at something, try saying I may not be an ace yet but I'll get there with consistent training, practice, and effort.

See what we've done there? We have simply replaced a negative notion with a hopeful and positive possibility. Overcome your fears or negative ideas about not being good at something. All experts have been novices in their field once upon a time. Let go of anxieties and fears, and actively participate with networking and social events.

If your goal is to give up a bad or self-destructive habit, have the confidence that you have the ability to do it. When your mind is overcome by negative and self-limiting beliefs, it becomes the reality of your subconscious mind. When your subconscious mind plays around with negative and self-limiting ideas, it is near impossible to align our actions positively towards the fulfillment of our goals.

6. Identify opportunities for personal growth. The most unfortunate thing in life about most people is they get comfortable doing what they are doing for a long time. It's like getting stuck in a rut. They are caught in the trap of their own comfort zones. Often, they don't want to move outside that comfort zone and discover their fullest potential.

When you move out of your comfort zone and seize opportunities that are different from what you've been doing, you give yourself a chance to explore your fullest potential. You never know how good you are at something unless you go out there and do it. "No guts no glory" is more than an adage.

Push the envelope once in a while and walk that extra mile if you really want to accomplish the glory you are destined for. Don't remain trapped in the cushy confines of your comfort zone. Extraordinary results can be accomplished only by doing extraordinary things. Be perceptive enough to seize fresh opportunities and options that add value to your personal development.

At times, due to our fear of change or overpowering feeling of uncertainty, we prevent ourselves from setting big or seemingly impossible goals. However, having a clear purpose is the first step towards accomplishing your goal. To identify a goal, you need to step outside your regular zone and be open to opportunities that contribute towards your personal development and growth.

7. Be ready for challenges. You should be someone who wholeheartedly embraces challenges as opportunities for growth. Set seemingly impossible or tough to accomplish goals and work towards them in a purposeful manner (more on this later). Never overlook the fact that you have the power within you to make a huge difference in this world. Yes, you have the power to create everything you want. There is a secret which I will share in the next chapter. A powerful secret that can help you internalize and manifest your goals!

Chapter 5: Programming Your Mind for Success

You know the chained elephant syndrome, right? The elephant is a powerful and mighty beast. With one tug of its strength, it can free itself from the chains and ropes that tie its legs to a tree. I mean, we are talking about the largest land mammal. However, it doesn't seem to make any effort to free itself from its chains and just stands there, tied, and resigned to its fate. Why? Because since the time the elephant was a baby, it was taught that it couldn't break free from the ropes and chains. Over a period of time, the powerful mammal believed this to be its truth. It could escape simply by showing some strength to shake off the chains. However, the most unfortunate thing is, it didn't know that it could break free from the chains, and therefore surrendered to its fate.

We are pretty much like the elephant. We have it in us to accomplish all the success, wealth, and glory we are destined to achieve. However, only a handful live a life of their dreams because the others, like the elephant, don't even know that they are capable of freeing themselves from their current, mediocre lives if they show the strength and fortitude to challenge their self-limiting beliefs.

Almost every success story starts with a mindset. All glorious people believe that they were destined to be rich and successful, which helps them actively work on their goals.

Carol Dweck, a Stanford psychologist, founded the "growth mindset and fixed mindset" concept in her book titled *Mindset: The New Psychology of Success*. One of the best takeaways from the book is that our mindset isn't some far-fetched abstract thought. It is a real concept that can nurtured to help you accomplish success, wealth and glory.

Do you possess the elephant's mindset that resigns to its destiny or do you possess a mindset that is constantly looking for opportunities and solutions to release yourself from the chains of a mediocre life to chase the exceptional and the extraordinary?

Which of the two mindsets you fall under will to a certain extent determine your chances of success and destiny. Debbie Millman aptly said, "If you imagine less, less will be what you undoubtedly deserve."

Plenty of research has been dedicated to the influence of thoughts and beliefs in our conscious as well as subconscious mind on our actions, and eventually destiny. We aren't as limited by our external circumstances as we are by a fixed mindset, which prevents us from moving outside our comfort zone.

The typical traits of a fixed mindset person are: they tend to believe everything from their intelligence to creativity to abilities is static. In their mind, it is impossible to transform, enhance, and sharpen it meaningfully to accomplish greater success. They operate with constricted beliefs that things can never get greater than they are. Everything is pre-determined and there is a huge fear of failure, which paralyzes them into inaction. This is their way of maintaining their current position, which prevents them from climbing greater heights of success. A typical fixed mindset stand is, "Oh! I'll appear completely foolish if I try something new and fail." This is a glaring fixed mindset philosophy.

The growth mindset doesn't hold a desire to be accepted or validated. It is more driven by a desire for passion, results, moving beyond one's comfort zone and taking calculated risks. Constantly pushing the envelope and raising the bar is the hallmark of a growth mindset. People with a fixed mindset don't believe in sticking to safe, cushy paths. Rather, they take on unexplored terrains that help them tap into their fullest potential and accomplish greater success.

Unfortunately, a majority of people don't even know that they are capable of accomplishing great success and wealth if they display the strength to act in the right direction. Don't be the elephant that is resigned to a less than glorious destiny. Gather the strength to move beyond past failures, self-limiting beliefs and other people's perception to achieve the greatness you are destined for and deserve.

Research has consistently pointed to the fact that positive thinking is more than being happy or displaying a characteristically cheerful attitude. Positive thinking can create real value and help you develop powerful life skills, which are much more than a smile or upbeat disposition. How does positive thinking influence our behavior? How can we harness the power of positive thinking to direct our behavior? What damage can negative thinking do to your actions? Read on to find out.

Thoughts Are the Key

Thoughts are the key factor influencing your behavior. It affects everything from how you feel to how you behave. For example, you may start your day thinking you are going to perform miserably at the interview later in the day. This causes a feeling of nervousness and stress, which directly affects your interview performance. Your thoughts have led to the belief that you aren't very likely to perform well at the interview. This manifests in your actions when you do not speak clearly or display confidence or do not sell yourself convincingly.

Your behavior only reinforces your thoughts of performing badly. The thought that you are not good enough gathers higher momentum. You are even more convinced about not being good enough and the connection between your thoughts and behavior is strengthened.

This premise is used to treat a variety of psychological issues including anxiety, depression, and stress. It can be used in corporate settings for enhancing performance, boosting leadership skills and increasing team spirit.

The Damaging Impact of Negative Thinking and a Fixed Mindset

Imagine this scenario. You are walking through a dense forest and are suddenly accosted by a wild beast right in your path. Your brain registers an immediate negative reaction. In this instance, it is fear. Studies have long proven that negative feelings program the human brain to perform a particular action. For example, when the wild beast comes in your path, you flee. You are completely focused on the beast, the fear it evokes in you, and how you can escape.

Negative emotions narrow down the focus of your thoughts. The brain cells ignore any alternatives such as climbing atop a tree, grabbing a stick, or playing dead. It simply concentrates on the problem or the beast staring you in the eye. This is exactly what negative thinking does to us in real world. It programs our brain to react to negative emotions in a limiting manner by shutting out positive alternatives.

For instance, rage and other emotions can consume you to such an extent that you cannot think rationally beyond it. Similarly, when you have a lot of things to do, you get into a paralytic mode, where you do not know where to begin. How do you feel when you do not exercise or eat healthy? You feel miserable about not having sufficient willpower, which only directs your behavior in the direction of laziness, creating more of the same behavior. Thus, thoughts create and influence our actions. We do what we think, and ultimately become what dominates our thoughts.

How Positive Thinking Impacts Positive Actions

Real positive thinking is not a few hours of feeling good. The greatest advantage of positive thinking is that it helps you build skills and resources for life. Barbara Fredrickson, a positive psychology researcher at the University of North Carolina has done plenty of research in the arena of using positive thinking to influence your life skills.

Fredrickson focuses on the "broaden and build" theory, which states that positive thoughts expand your sense of possibilities and broaden your thinking. It lets you create new resources and skill sets that offer real value in different spheres of life. In complete contrast, negative thinking only focuses on tackling an immediate threat, such as the beast in the earlier example. It does not concentrate on building skills that are valuable in future.

It is rightfully said that thoughts build your character. It determines how an individual operates in the world and how a person conducts himself physically, emotionally, and spiritually. You are an aggregation of everything you think and every action originates from your thoughts. Your inner thinking directly influences in your external circumstances. Self-induced changes are often precluded by changes in our thinking pattern. For instance, if you want to give up a bad habit, it has to originate from a shift in your thoughts. You must first identify its ill effects and resolve to give it up before you actually go about abstaining from it.

Consider this scientific principle behind how our thoughts can actually affect our behavior. Each thought releases some brain chemicals. Negative thinking drains the mind from a feel-good forcefulness. It slows down the mind, dims the mind's capacity to function and induces a feeling of depression. Positive thoughts, on the other hand, decrease the quantity of cortisol (stress-inducing chemical) and boosts the production of serotonin (creates a feeling of well-being). This also helps your mind function at its optimal capacity.

Train Your Brain for Positive Thoughts

The actions we perform are known to expand or shrink different brain regions. The more you direct your brain to perform, the more its cortical space expands to tackle new jobs. It develops stronger connections within spaces that emphasize on desired behavior patterns or thoughts while weakening the link with others. Thus, we are what we think and feel. Whatever we think or say is directly evident in our behavior. What we become outside is a direct outcome of what we believe/think inside, which means our brain can be trained to think more positively.

Start by tuning your mind towards happy thoughts. Learn to look at the brighter side of things. Refocus your brain when negative thoughts rear their ugly head. Your mind is in complete control of your thoughts. You are in the driver's seat controlling the direction of your thoughts. Your thoughts have the power to determine what you create in life. Use these thoughts to your advantage by reframing circumstances/events and thinking positively. Positive thinking shouldn't simply be a feel-good or temporary optimism syndrome. Make it a life philosophy. Incorporate positive thinking in your lifestyle to witness its benefits in helping you lead a rewarding, fulfilling and gratifying life.

Do you know you have a magic weapon that can help you accomplish everything you want? Yes, practically everything! It can help you fulfill all your objectives, desires, goals and visions. The magic tool is capable of converting your thoughts into tangible things. Your ideas into reality! Your visions into your destiny! This all-powerful and potent tool is none other than your subconscious mind.

Our subconscious mind has the potential to fulfill all our desires. It has the power to absorb ideas we feed into it and guide our actions in alignment with these ideas. The superpower of our subconscious mind is it cannot differentiate between the real and imagined. For instance, if you keep visualizing yourself as a rich and successful person, the mind doesn't recognize this as wishful thinking. It firmly believes this to be your reality.

Once the subconscious mind believes something to be real, it leads your actions in line with you it believes. If your mind believes you are a rich and successful go-getter, it will seize opportunities, come up with ideas and lead you to take action in the direction of success. You have the power to create everything you desire with the help of your subconscious mind.

The human mind consists of three layers, the conscious, subconscious and unconscious mind. While the conscious mind is a realm we are fully aware of, we have almost no awareness of the thoughts, feelings, emotions, beliefs and ideas held within subconscious and unconscious (which is what makes it so powerful).

Thus, we often hold certain strong positive, negative, self-limiting, and empowering ideas within our subconscious unknowingly. Since this realm of your mind remains inaccessible, you don't know what thoughts and beliefs are held in it, which are impacting your actions.

However, the good news is, you can start feeding empowering and positive ideas to your subconscious mind by internalizing your goals. When you internalize your goals, the subconscious mind believes it to be your reality. When it believes something to be your ultimate reality, it guides your actions in alignment with these positive and empowering thoughts.

You possess all the resources and tools to make a roaring success of your life. You have the potential to manifest any goal or dream because you choose what you feed into your subconscious mind.

Chances are you've already heard about Rhonda Byrne's book and movie *The Secret?* If no, here's a quick summary. It is based on the law of attraction, which borrows from multiple fields of study such as quantum physics, metaphysics, psychology, spirituality, and more. In short, the law of attraction states that we have the ability to create our reality through our thoughts, which are believed to hold powerful energy frequencies. When we transit these thoughts into the realm of the universe, the universe energy (or atomic mass of energy held within the universal space and time) responds to our thoughts with a matching frequency to give us exactly what we want.

Think of yourself as nothing but a bundle of energy, pretty similar to everything in the universe. You act as an energy magnet, which thought-feelings, thoughts, emotions, and actions is attracting things in your life. When the universal atoms or energy receives these energy signals, it responds with a frequency match and you receive exactly what you fixate your feelings and thoughts on.

This unfortunately works both ways. The universal energy cannot distinguish between the positive and negative. It doesn't know what's good or not good for you. It simply responds at an energy level. I've had people come up to me and ask why despite the best efforts they aren't able to manifest their desires. The problem is easy to pin down.

A majority of times, we end up focusing on what we want to get rid of or what we want to avoid instead of what we want. When you focus on what you want to discard instead of what you wish to attract, you end up attracting even more of the unwanted because that's where your thought energy is concentrated.

Let's say I want to be wealthy. My dream is to earn plenty of money and live a life free of insecurity, debt, and financial burdens. Instead of channelizing my thoughts in the direction of "being wealthy", if I focus on "don't want to be poor", I'll only end up attracting more poverty. The universe doesn't understand the difference between negatives and positives. It will give you what you ask for, so better focus on and ask for the right things. One of the most common reasons why we can't accomplish true success is because we focus on what we want to eliminate instead of what we want to magnetize in our life.

Remember, you have the key to fulfill your goals by reprogramming your mind and transmitting the perfect energy signals to the universe so you can use the law of attraction for your goal fulfillment.

Visualization

Practice visualization techniques on awakening or before hitting the bed each day. Our subconscious mind is at its active best when the conscious mind rests while we are asleep. This is why most of our "aha moments" or "moments of solutions and realizations" happen while we are asleep.

Visualizing just before you go to bed helps you mind absorb these images clearly and work on them. Begin by sitting in a distraction-free space, which has a positive, relaxed, and calming aura. Sit in a comfortable position and close your eyes. You will now imagine or visualize powerful images through your mind's eye.

Begin by visualizing what you want in absolute and vivid details. Remember, the more precise, detailed, and unambiguous your visualization, the higher are your chances of manifesting it. You are telling your subconscious mind exactly what you desire to receive from a catalog of goodies. Make your visualization a multi-sensory process.

Let us say you are visualizing your dream office. Imagine it in explicit, graphic, and multi-sensory details. How does the entrance of your office look? What is the logo and text on the board at the entrance? How does your workplace smell? What color are the walls? How are the tables, chairs, and other furniture? What's the flooring like? How are the windows and doors like? Visualize everything in detail.

Similarly, if your goal is to make become a millionaire at the end of the year, visualize being a millionaire. How do you look as a millionaire? What are the clothes, footwear, and accessories you are sporting? How do people respond to you? How do people greet you when they meet you for the first time? How to do walk, talk, stand, and express yourself?

By imagining all this in detail, you are allowing your subconscious mind to internalize these powerful goals and guide your actions in line with these goals. The most important aspect of visualization is to imagine them as if these are your reality (or as if they've already been fulfilled), happening in your life currently, not as something you want in future.

You must align your thought energy with the idea that this is indeed your reality. By going over these positive thoughts repeatedly, you are building powerful ideas and energy vibrations that invariably help you magnetize these things. Wishful thinking doesn't work because when you operate from the perspective of wanting something, you are confirming the lack of it in your life presently. However, when you operate from the perspective that something is already yours, you are simply drawing more of it.

For instance, let us say you want to be rich and lead a financially secure and comfortable life. When you focus on wanting more, you are in effect stating that you don't have enough of it.

Visualizing from this from a scarcity of wealth and prosperity perspective makes it even more scarce and unattainable.

However, if you operate from the perspective of already possessing plenty of wealth and prosperity, you are on your way to attracting more riches and a financially glowing fortune. Imagine, visualize, and internalize the emotions and feelings of achieving your goals. Practice visualize for a minimum of 10 minutes two times a day.

When you strongly imprint strong ideas of being rich, successful, and productive in your subconscious mind, you program is for recognizing and seizing opportunities that create even greater wealth and success (or other goals you may have).

Focus your thoughts on positivity, action, gratitude and prosperity, while eliminating negative, self-limiting and anxious thoughts that act as obstacles to your success.

By concentrating on what you desire as if you already own it, you are tuning your mind to new possibilities, perspectives, and opportunities. Leverage the characteristic of your subconscious mind where the line between reality and imagined reality is blurred. Your feelings and emotions about the goals you desire to accomplish is the most powerful magnet when it comes to magnetizing these goals. Our feelings possess energy that is communicating with the universe at an atomic level. Overpoweringly positive feelings about accomplishing your goal helps you act in line with this belief.

Through the process of visualization, you are feeding tangible ideas to the subconscious mind or clear, conspicuous goals to work on. Visualization helps you identify and clarify your goals, while keeping these images active in your subconscious to lead you into taking positive action in the direction of these goals.

By practicing consistent visualization, your thoughts, emotions and feelings stay in alignment with your goals. This helps you stay motivated, positive and inspired. Visualization is a multi-disciplinary technique that can channelize your mental power to convert your goals or visions into tangible reality.

I also recommend combining the practice of visualization with mediation, deep breathing, and guided visualization (there are plenty of guided visualization videos on the internet).

One of the most important things to keep in mind when it comes to internalizing your goals through visualization is to view yourself as an active participant in it. Let's say you are viewing the movie of your life. However, you aren't just a passive audience who is watching events unfold before you. You are the main character, an active participant, and an integral part of the movie. You visualize yourself living your goals in different settings. You feel, imagine and absorb all experiences, including the sensory ones.

Once your subconscious mind absorbs all goals, it'll be easier to work in line with these goals.

Affirmations

Affirmations are powerful positive statements that are uttered repetitively to help implant an idea or goal into the subconscious mind. This process then enables the subconscious mind to believe these ideas/goals, and align your actions in line with them. The key is to keep saying these statements aloud or writing them continuously for the subconscious to accept it as your ultimate reality.

When we say something repeatedly, our words have tremendous impact on the subconscious mind. There are certain energy vibrations associated with specific words, which create either positive and empowering mental images or negative and defeatist images. The energy frequency we feed our mind through words and phrases we continuously use ultimately impact our actions. Thus, by feeding it empowering mental images, we are channelizing our subconscious mind for success, wealth and life mastery.

Start this right away. Begin by creating a positive statement about an aspect of your life you wish you change. For instance, if you want to develop a more proactive, go-getter attitude when it comes to recognizing and seizing opportunities, try saying, "I am a proactive and action-oriented person who is always ready to identify and embrace new opportunities."

Similarly, if you want to make money your affirmation can be something along the lines of, "I am a powerful money magnet. Money comes to me effortlessly." If you want to develop greater confidence or self-assertiveness, say something like, "I am a self-assured, assertive and confident person who has command over people and situations."

Say your affirmations for a minimum of three times a day, 20 times each (60 times in total). You'll gradually begin to notice a change in the way you view yourself, your situation or your chances of success. There will be a greater feeling of positivity and confidence in fulfilling your goals. Check your feelings, beliefs, and emotions before sleeping each night. Do you notice a difference after using affirmations? Do you feel more aligned with your goals? Do you feel the positive energy of these highly potent words and phrases? Is there a greater sense of hopefulness, optimism and positive energy? The answer is a resounding yes!

Affirmations are designed to keep our subconscious mind stay concentrated on our goals. They help keep the mind on track with empowering thoughts, ideas and energy to restrict doubts, self-limiting beliefs, fears and other negative thought energy vibrations. When we realize our true potential, we have the power to activate the dormant goal-fulfilling powers of our subconscious. Notice the changes when you start saying your affirmations. You'll begin to feel more enthusiastic, energized, and inspired about accomplishing them. There has to be a positive transformation from within to experience a transformation outside.

Before creating your affirmations, focus on what exactly you want to accomplish. Clarifying our goal makes it easy to internalize the goal to accomplish exactly what we want. Also, keep all affirmations in present tense. You shouldn't say them as something that you hope to accomplish in future. It should be said as your current reality. For instance, "I am rich, wealthy, and prosperous."

Similarly, do not use negative words or phrases. Your subconscious mind as well as the universe doesn't understand "no" "not" "never" etc. Instead of saying, "I don't want to be in debt" say "I am wealthy and financially-free." Focus on statements that assert what you want not what you wish to get rid of. Also avoid using words or phrases such as "I wish for", "I seek" or "I desire/want." This again shifts the focus to the lack of it in your life currently. Always affirm in present, doing, thinking and being what you truly desire.

Be very specific about what you want. Imagine the universe to be a catalog of desires or wishes. If you place a vague order, you may not receive your product or you'll end up receiving another product that you didn't want.

This is exactly how the universe responds to your desires. Keep your affirmations precise, unambiguous and to the point. If you want to increase your monthly income, simply stating that "my monthly income has risen" may not have the desired effect. Even a raise of $0.50 is an increase, right? Instead, if we say, "My monthly income has risen by $1,000", we are giving our mind a clear figure to work with. Thus the feeling that are earning $1,000 more each month is internalized, driving our subconscious mind to work on the goal effectively. Mention your affirmations in exacts to boost your chances of accomplishing it.

Eliminate every ounce of doubt, uncertainty, and insecurity held within you while chanting your affirmations. The intention should be positive and hopeful. Do not let your mind be overcome by fear of failure or other negative thoughts. You must believe these statements to be your truth for the law of attraction to work. A highly positive and potent energy frequency will be sent into the universe when you say these statements with a powerful intention. We must also believe that we are truly deserving of the wealth, success, and mastery that we desire. Our goal magnetizing energy increases when we believe ourselves to be worthy of receiving everything we want.

There are tons of examples where people do not enjoy fulfilling and healthy interpersonal relationships in life or always end up falling in love with the wrong people and getting hurt repeatedly. If they do a mental check-in, they'll realize the root cause. They do not believe they deserve to be a loving and healthy relationship to begin with. When we don't believe you deserve something, we are blocking its energy into our life by creating negative thought energy around it.

Do not block the energy for magnetizing your goals by doubting your worthiness to accomplish it. The best time to say your affirmations is when you are facing the mirror while shaving, applying make-up, getting dressed, and so on. Observe the feelings, expressions and energy vibrations your experience while saying your affirmations.

I also like to stick my affirmations in places where I can prominently spot it throughout the day. There are these colorful, little post-it notes that have my affirmations on them, which I've stuck throughout my home and office. I read them mentally or aloud each time I come across them. You can stick your affirmations on the bathroom mirror, refrigerator, kitchen cabinets, cupboards, computer, and work desk—just about any place where you can see them several times in a day. We are doing nothing but embedding these ideas in our subconscious mind to draw it into action mode.

Feel the energy and emotions of your words while saying them rather than chanting them in a mechanical, auto-pilot manner.

Internalize the emotions and feelings attached to the words. For example, if you state you are a money magnet who is forever attracting wealth and riches, soak in the emotions of being rich and prosperous. This is the key to activating the power of your subconscious mind and the law of attraction.

Journaling

Journaling is another powerful habit if you want to fulfill your life goals. The physical act of writing sends intensely strong signals to our subconscious to bring our actions in line with what we write.

Keep a goal, gratitude, dream, or stream of consciousness journal. Gratitude is one of the most power-packed emotions when it comes to multiplying your blessings. In the book *Magic*, bestselling manifestation author Rhonda Byrne writes about the power of gratitude and thankfulness in attracting our goals or increasing more of the good things we possess.

Do this small exercise starting today. Mention a list of ten things that happened during your day that you are grateful for before going to bed each night. You can also create a list of ten things that you are blessed to have in your life each night. Ensure that it's a different list each day without any repetitions. Each day, challenge yourself to come up with ten new things that you are thankful for. Think there aren't that many? You'll be surprised.

Mention everything from your eyes to your Wi-Fi connection to the roof above your head to your hands to the food—there's a lot to be thankful for. Irrespective of your present situation, be thankful for all you have. When we express thankfulness for what we already have, we transmit a powerful, positive energy into the realm of the universe, which true to its nature sends us even more of what we are thankful for.

If you want to attract more wealth, express gratefulness for your current wealth! If you want a pay hike, begin by being thankful for what you currently make.

Imagine your blessings while mentioning them in the gratitude journal. Thank the universe or any other force of your choice for these blessings while writing them. Similar to affirmations and visualizations, journal your goals as if they are already fulfilled.

We invest most of our time soaking in our problems and challenges. Understand that problems are a huge sign of life, that you are living and doing things. Perhaps the only time someone is problem-free is when they are six feet beneath. Shift focus from your problems to blessings. If you want to attract things you are grateful for, begin by expressing gratitude for existing blessings. Be grateful for everything, including your problems and challenges.

Gratitude is the biggest pathway to happiness, glowing health, and success. It shifts our energy and attention from what we lack to what we have, which in turn helps us materialize greater blessings. It's the abundance of small pleasures, joys, and opportunities that we take for granted.

Write how it feels to accomplish your goals, the feelings, and emotions you experience after accomplishing your goals, and other details in the present tense. The subconscious mind will believe everything to be true, and help you act in line with your writings. Thus your actions are guided by a more proactive and action-oriented thought process.

One of the most effective ways to unravel feelings, emotions, and thoughts held in our subconscious (often the self-limiting beliefs, fears and insecurities we hold within our subconscious prevents us from accomplishing our goals) is to write in a stream of consciousness. Write thoughts that freely flow through the stream of your consciousness without restraining, editing, or assessing them. The act should be more intuitive and spontaneous, almost like an involuntary and uncontrollable impulse. You'll be surprised to learn about the thoughts, ideas, and beliefs held in your subconscious.

I also recommend keeping a dream journal handy next to your bed to tap into the subconscious. As soon as you awake after a dream or in the morning, start writing about your dream in detail along with the feelings you experienced while going through it. The idea is to put everything on paper before you forget it. Identify if there's a recurring pattern through your dreams. Accessing the ideas held in your subconscious through your dreams gives you the power to modify these ideas and beliefs if they aren't in line with your goal fulfillment.

Once our conscious realm takes precedence on awakening, the thoughts and ideas of the subconscious fade away, which is why it is important to note down your dreams quickly. Observe if there are any negative, defeatist, or self-limiting thought patterns revealed through your dreams? Is there a recurring theme in a majority of your dreams? These are most likely our innermost thoughts, ideas and beliefs that stop us from accomplishing our goals. The transition from procrastination or inaction to hustling or productivity becomes smoother when you replace negative and self-limiting thoughts with positive, empowering and constructive ideas, thoughts and beliefs. This is the key to internalizing your goals and donning the success mindset.

The habit of writing a daily journal is extremely therapeutic. It helps a person release negative thoughts such as regret, anger, low self-worth, stress, anxiety, and so on. Releasing these thoughts is integral to the process of slipping into a more winning, goal-fulfilling mindset. Journaling is a wonderful way to eliminate potential blocks that can come in the way of your goals.

Make your journal as personalized and relevant as you like. It should be a reflection of your unique personality and goals. Add stickers, comic strips, movie quotes, lines from your favorite books, photographs, ticket stubs, feathers, sketches, doodles, or anything that bets represents your goals to make the journal more personalized, meaningful and connect-worthy. You should feel an instant connect with your journal.

Don't simply write your goals and forget about it. The process of writing of course has plenty of advantages. However, go over your journal entries periodically to track your thoughts, feelings, beliefs, and emotions. You may notice a transformation in your thought patterns and beliefs. At the end of each week and month, go over all the entries for the particular week and month. Leave some space for reflecting upon your progress.

Make a Vision Board

This one's my favorite. It now just helps you clarify your goals but also uses the power of your subconscious mind in manifesting these goals. Visuals have a strong impact on our subconscious mind. When it keeps seeing a visual or image repeatedly, the subconscious mind believes that to be your reality. It fantastically aligns your personal energy to the process of fulfilling your goals.

A vision board is a board that holds images or visuals of all your desires, goals, visions, dreams, and objectives. Visuals are said to have a far more powerful impact on our subconscious than words. It is the difference between telling your mind what you want and showing it what you want. As simple as that! When our subconscious is exposed to a visual continuously, it internalizes the idea and believes it to be real. This helps our subconscious align our actions in line with these empowering visuals to facilitate goal fulfillment.

Be creative while making your vision board. It should be fun, personal, and meaningful. Make a collage of images and photographs that resonate with your goals. It can be images from a catalog, brochure, magazine, internet, and comic strip—anything that symbolizes your goals pictorially. Select images that "talk to you" about your goals. Use your own photographs to reinforce goals. For instance, if you want to travel often, use a picture of one of your most memorable trips. The idea is to feed exactly what you want to accomplish in your subconscious mind. Who needs a genie with a magic lamp when you have your subconscious mind?

Place your vision board in a position where it's the first thing you see before you hit the bed and on waking up each morning. Place it on a wall opposite your bed. The vision board can also be placed above your work desk.

Notice how our conscious mind can seldom come up with solutions and ideas that the subconscious is capable of creating while we are asleep. Avoid picking pictures hurriedly or on a whim. Use only those visuals that resonate with you at a deeper level. Experience the emotions attached to these visuals, and feel them at a deeper level.

Avoid cluttering your vision board with too many images at once. Stick to four or five images at a time to help your mind focus clearly on them. You can also create a different vision board for each theme; say a wealth and career vision board, a relationship vision board and so on. Much like the journal, you can use a variety of elements to add more character to your vision board or personalize it. Souvenirs, tickets, pebbles, jewelry – anything that makes it unique, personal, and stunning!

Turning Negative Self-talk into Positive Self-Talk

Your mental chatter to a large extent determines your destiny. If this seems like an exaggerated statement—think again. Our subconscious is slowly but surely absorbing our mental conversations to create our thoughts, beliefs, ideas, and attitude. When you talk to yourself as a "loser who can never get anything right" this is exactly what you are imprinting in the subconscious.

Again, it guides your action from this self-limiting and defeatist point of view. This is why it is said, "Whether you think you can or you can't—you are right." This is because whatever you think is what your mind is going to create or lead you into doing. We blame everyone from the people we work with to our circumstances to our destiny for our failures without doing a mental check-in on the ideas we hold about self through our self-talk.

Worry not if aren't exactly your own cheerleader. I've got your back covered there, too. Here are some of the most powerful ways through which you can go from being a self-loathing critic to your biggest cheerleader.

1. Identify your thought patterns. What is the first thought that occurs to you when your boss summons you and says he/she needs to speak to urgently. I am going to be fired? I must have done something really bad? The project that I submitted last evening is below his/her expectations? I mean you'd never really think, he/she's called you to ask if you are ready to accept more responsibility by taking up a big, upcoming project.

That's the thing about our thoughts. They are uncontrollable and involuntary. You don't have a mental leash to tame them. They automatically pop into your head without any effort.

From now on, I want you to closely monitor your inner dialogues. Take a few minutes to evaluate your conversation with yourself on a daily basis. Is there a clear pattern emerging through it? Do you always see yourself as victim of circumstances? Do you always doubt your ability to do things? Do you think you are unworthy or incapable of accomplish success and wealth? Are your opinions about yourself based on what other people think about you? There is almost always a clear underlying current in our negative self-dialogue. Recognizing this issue and eliminating it is the key to becoming your own cheerleader. Get into the habit of monitoring your habits consciously to identify unrealistic, irrational, self-limiting, and unproductive thoughts.

2. Look for evidence of thoughts being true and untrue. Just because you think something doesn't necessarily mean it is true. Often our self-limiting beliefs, thoughts, and ideas are not facts but merely opinions. They aren't necessarily true. Each time you find yourself engaging in negative inner dialogue, look for evidence of its accuracy. Ask yourself, "What is the evidence that makes this thought true?" Going back to the above example, do you have evidence that your boss is going to fire you?

3. Make a list of all evidence that backs up your thoughts. You may have missed a crucial deadline or stayed absent from work

for days due to illness! List every reason why you think you are about to be fired.

Now create a list of reasons why your thoughts hold no value. You may be one of the team's most efficient and hardest workers. Clients request that you take on their projects because you are known to be a competent worker who delivers above average results! You've been called to meet the boss urgently on earlier occasions too without being fired.

If you have trouble coming up with evidence contrary to your negative chatter, ask yourself if you'd say the same thing to a close friend with the same issue. What would you say to him or her in a similar situation? If your friend calls and says, "Know what? I am about to be fired. What would your reaction be? You'll come up with a bunch of reasons why they won't be fired. Give yourself the same pep talk and consolation each time you find yourself engaging in negative self-talk.

4. Reframe your words and thoughts. When you've looked at a situation from both angles, create more realistic and less catastrophic statement about it. Instead of saying, "my boss wants to fire me because I goofed up on the last project" try telling yourself "yes, I goofed up on the last project but there are

several other reasons why my boss would want to talk to me." It'll help things stay in the right perspective.

I wouldn't recommend convincing yourself in too positive or glowing terms either when it comes to challenging negative self-talk. You'll know you are lying in you can't play football and think you are "the next Cristiano Ronaldo."

Stop thinking in extremes and look for more realistic thought patterns to move from inertia to productivity.

5. How bad is bad really? Okay so maybe your boss does want to fire you or you may not succeed in your next business venture if you try. How bad is that? Spend a few minutes thinking about your response. Okay, maybe I am not good at this. What does that mean? I can never be good at it?

The consequences are often not as drastic as we imagine them to be. Much like when someone doesn't respond to our calls or texts, in our signature catastrophic thinking patterns we believe the person is ignoring us or is with someone more interesting. Things aren't as bad a majority of the times. Negative thought patterns are wired in the human brain since evolution. Sensing danger and unfortunate events comes to us easily. However, that doesn't mean everything bad is going to happen to you all the time.

Think about all the times you've not done something out of a compelling fear of failure. Didn't you regret it later when you witnessed others making a roaring success of it? Even if you fail, is it the end of the world? If you are fired, there are other companies and jobs to apply for.

If you fail at a start-up (you won't really know until you try, would you?), there are other businesses to venture into. You have options. Remind yourself that eventually everything is alright. Put a pause on the anxiety, panic and worry button immediately.

You may never completely get rid of negative self-chatter, which is alright. The idea is to understand the brain's conclusions, remarks, and predictions aren't always accurate, and our actions are often based on these inaccurate beliefs, conclusions, or predictions. This way, you won't tend to be too affected by your negative self-chatter that often stirs up unproductive actions. The practice of replacing negative dialogues or self-talk with more positive ideas equips you to reach your fullest potential. You will less likely to be the best version of yourself if you keep talking down to yourself or beating yourself up mentally.

Avoid the urge to drag yourself down all the time but instead, make your mental chatter more productive, uplifting, and realistic. This makes all the difference when it comes to internalizing your goals. Remember Brain Tracy's 10 percent rule? Just begin and accomplish 10 percent of your task to sustain the goal over a period of time. You are less likely to quit if you pick up the right momentum by completing 10 percent of the task.

Chapter 6: Self-Discipline

You understand by now why habits and self-discipline in so vital to your success and how delaying gratification while keeping your eyes firmly on the larger goal takes you closer to them. Here are some powerful tips for growing your self-discipline superpower.

1. Have a clear sense of purpose. This isn't rocket science. When you have a clear sense of purpose about why you want to do

something, you're definitely more invested in the daily grind and challenges of accomplishing it. Have a bigger, clear purpose for everything you do from getting a degree to signing up for a public speaking class. Keep your eyes on the bigger picture will become easier. Haven't you heard motivation speaker say, when your way is clear, the how will invariably find a way. Knowing your purpose is the key to identifying the direction to get there.

2. Develop perseverance. Yes, the tough indeed get going when the going gets tough. Frustration and a feeling of hopeless can drive the best of us to quit. But those who don't emerge doubly victorious! Don't view tough situations as something that are happening "to you." Rather view them as something that are happening "for you." This will change your mindset.

Challenges add value to your life rather than taking away from you. You learn to adapt, sustain, and accommodate, which in turn builds your success muscle. When there is an obstacle in your path, you'll look for another route rather than halting the journey. Remember, setbacks are permanent circumstances meant to stop your progress. They are temporary situations that can be used to empower you. Strengthen your resolve and keep going, success may be much closer than you believe.

3. Spend time on productive tasks. Ever wondered why when everyone has 24 hours in day, someone people manage to pack so much into them while others barely scrap through? Time management, increasing productivity, and eliminating distractions is the key. You choose what you spend your time and energy on. If you choose to allow virtual games and social media to consume your day, you've been unproductive (unless you are planning to build your own game or social media app now don't use that as an excuse).

Always ask yourself if what you are investing your time and energy on is valuable to your goal? Does it take you closer to your goal? Does it have a positive impact on the fulfillment of your goal? If not, find other things to focus on!

4. Don't dwell on past mistakes. This is another mindset change you should develop in your pursuit for self-discipline. Many people are so consumed by their past mistakes that they fail to look into or create a future of their dreams. Overlook these mistakes and move ahead. Things won't always go according to a fixed plan. There will be setbacks, which you need to take in the right spirit and move on.

Rather than being enveloped by guilt, regret, remorse, frustration, and anger, channelize your energies productively towards the future. Forgive yourself for past mistakes and get back into the game. The longer you take off from the game to dwell on past mistakes, the harder it is going to be for you to sustain your efforts in a positive direction.

5. Eat Healthy. Eating healthy is the key to being more energetic, keeping fit, feeling good, and being more active. Food substances that are greasy, heavy, and high on bad fats will make you feel lethargic and drain your energy. More energy is consumed in burning high calories foods, which means you are left with virtually energy for productive tasks.

Avoid eating sugar, artificially sweeteners, processed/canned food, and nutrition-free junk food that doesn't add value to your body. Instead, stick to freshly cooked food or raw fruits/vegetables that are high in vitamin and mineral content. They will provide your body the necessary nutrition and energy to stay active and focused. When you eat right, you feel right. And we know how important feeling right is if you want to achieve success.

Develop healthy eating habits such as eating in small portions frequently rather than eating few large meals. Keep fixed hours for meals no matter how busy you are. Keep your fueled throughout the day with healthy and nutritious snacks.

6. Understand that it is alright to fail if you put in your best. Every effort may not get you a shiny trophy but hey, there are several lessons you'll learn along the way. I mean, at best you'll now know what not to do to get the desired result. The end result isn't important all the time. Enjoy the journey of learning and the passion of taking on varied challenges to test your potential. There will be room for improvement all the time. Let that not deter you from pursuing further.

Stop worrying about other people's judgments and perceptions. Put in your best and learn how to get better than the best in future! At times, it's worth your while to focus on the experience rather than end result. Learn to substitute the word failing with enlightenment or learning. Value the journey rather than the end result or destination.

7. Master your attitude. This is not just other fancy tee slogan. You attitude defines the outcome you'll experience in life. Keep it positive, passionate, hungry and stimulating. Take

responsibility for your actions rather than blaming circumstances. Be proactive and seek opportunities. When life closes one door, push open another! A winsome attitude is what differentiates average from the exceptional!

While everyone is capable of accomplishing success and greatness, not everyone does. Ever wondered why? Simple. They just don't have the attitude for success. Flex your growth muscle by working on your attitude right away.

8. Dream. Every act of glory, every success story, every account of greatness began with a dream as Walt Disney famously remarked, "All our dreams can come true if we have the courage to pursue them." Avoid placing restrictions or limitations on your dreams. Don't say, "LOL, I am an intern. There's no way I am going to head this company in a couple of years" because you know what, this may unfortunately come true! Embrace your dreams and work actively towards fulfilling them, a step at a time. "If you aim for the moon, you'll land on the stars."

9. Eliminate temptations. The pursuit of self-control becomes easier when you stick to the "out of sight is out of mind" adage. Remove temptations, distractions, and pointless activities that do not contribute positively to your goal from your immediate

environment. If you are trying to spend more time studying, cancel your Netflix subscription. If you want greater control over eating habits, don't store junk food.

If you find yourself being distracted by your phone messenger while completing a task, switch it off or keep it away. An app like SelfControl can be downloaded to block out distracting websites for a given period. Ditching negative influences and temptations is setting yourself up for success.

10. Develop critical thinking. Be inquisitive. Build a mindset of curiosity rather than accepting things as they are. Learn to question ideas rather than simply letting them go unchallenged. Much like a test, you can mug up your lessons and score an A. However, it won't be lesson you can successfully implement. Attempt to learn why things are the way they are. Go beyond the obvious or what is expected from you and come up with different ways to do things.

Developing critical thinking will allow you to look beyond obvious ideas and solutions to come up with something path-breaking. It will make you more solution oriented. You'll learn to use your reasoning powers for thinking of new ways to do things.

11. Work on yourself. You are a work in progress and not a completed piece (not to be mistaken for you are incomplete). Change thought patterns that overemphasize on perfection, happiness, comfort, security, and smartness. Tell yourself it is alright to feel uncomfortable and imperfect sometimes. Keep working on developing new skills, open yourself to new ideas, identify areas that you can improve upon and basically like your favorite software, keep coming up with upgraded versions of yourself. Remember, you are a work in progress and not a finished product. The day you think you know everything is the day your downfall begins.

12. Exercise regularly. That does a lot of good for your mind and body is no secret. However, it also teaches you some vital lessons on your path to success. Other than looking fit and feeling good about yourself, you'll pick up vital skills such as self-control, restraint, getting comfortable with the idea of being uncomfortable, pushing yourself, and demonstrating resilience.

A regular exercise routine leads to the secretion of endorphins in the brain and nervous system, thus allowing us to experience more positive feelings. And we could all use a little positivity to achieve success, right?

13. Sleep well. Trust me on this, you're never going to get enough done if you don't eat and sleep well. You may lead yourself to believe that you are accomplishing a lot by skipping lunch or giving up on your sleep but it'll backfire sooner than you realize. How you treat your body now is how you will be treated by your body a few years down the line.

Grab at least 7-8 hours of undisturbed sleep every day. To enjoy a peaceful sleep, avoid watching gadgets at least 2 hours before hitting the bed. Keep the television out of your bedroom. Sleep and awake at a fixed time every day to keep a more disciplined body clock. Develop a relaxing routine just before going to bed. Don't use your bed for anything other than sleeping and intimate encounters.

Keep the atmosphere in your bedroom soothing, relaxing, comfortable, and temperature-controlled. Minimize your exposure to bright, powerful light post evening time. Turn off all gadgets an hour prior to sleeping if possible. Avoid consuming a hearty meal or caffeine just before hitting the bed. Notice how irritable and snappy you become when you don't get enough sleep. This won't help you focus, which eventually saps your productivity.

14. Use it breaks and rewards too. All discipline and no play can indeed make Jack (or Jill) a dull boy. You can't run 100 miles at once. You need to break your journey into bits and take breaks too for replenishing your energy and senses. If you try to work non-stop, you will burn out. Exhaustion and stress overcome your nerves and you will be forced to give up. The smarter way of covering a long journey is to take periodic breaks and reward yourself for covering every milestone.

15. Develop good habits. Once we keep performing an act over and over again, it becomes a habit. And the best or worst part about habits (depending on whether they are good or bad) is it becomes almost involuntary since they are a result of neurological cravings.

We have little control over our habits once they become a part of us. Therefore, take your bad habits head on and start developing more positive habits that add value to your goals. Get rid of negative habits by eliminating your triggers, establishing positive routine, and using rewards for practicing positive habits. Exercise self-control and restraint by focusing on the bigger picture.

16. Anticipate potential challenges and beat them using strategic methods. Whether you are trying to give up a negative habit or develop more positive habits in your pursuit for self-discipline, anticipate obstacles on the path. However, stay a step ahead of these supposed challenges by having a ready plan of action. Let's say, you plan to flex your muscles at the gym every morning in a bid to get fitter.

However, you already know each time your alarm rings, you hit snooze and go right back to bed. What are the things you can do to force yourself to rise early and workout at the gym? Try keeping the alarm on the other side of the room so you're forced to walk up to it and turn it off. Once you make the effort to walk, you'll be fully awake and less likely to go back to bed.

Similarly, if you want to give up drinking alcohol and you know your favorite bar is on way back from work, you can decide to take a different route to avoid slipping back to your old ways. Think of strategic solutions for potential self-discipline challenges.

Don't go drill sergeant on yourself all the time. Combat stress, boredom, and exhaustion with relaxing and fun breaks. Every once in a while allow yourself to do something fun and relaxing.

Schedule breaks in between tasks. Reward yourself each time you complete a milestone or successfully resist temptation.

Rewards and treats work wonderfully well when you are trying to break a bad habit or develop more positive habits. If you want to lose weight, treat yourself to a relaxing massage for every successful month of working out in the gym. Similarly, reserve Sundays for ice-cream of your favorite cup of coffee. Rewards and positive reinforcements help you stay motivated towards your goal, while also making the process more fun and less challenging.

17. Build connections and conversations with new people rather than hanging out with the same set of people who limit your thoughts and actions. Stay open-minded, learn new things from these people, and ready yourself for challenges. In shorten, periodically fresh up and stimulate your life with new people. People who keep learning never stop growing. They are constantly evolving and developing.

18. Meditate. Lo and behold, I am not advocating some spiritual mumbo-jumbo here. All I am doing is urging you to use meditation for disciplining your mind, body, and spirit. Meditation helps you develop greater control, clarity, and focus.

It helps you penetrate into different layers of your mind (the subconscious and unconscious) to help you connect with deeper thoughts (subsequently challenge and change self-limiting notions). You develop greater mindfulness and awareness of your environment, and your resistance power becomes stronger. Don't make it a full-fledged ritual. Keep it simple yet effective. It can be anything you want it to be instead of being a rigid, must-follow ritual.

Practice deep breathing by being more mindful of your breath to the count of 1-10 in a peaceful environment. Focus on your breath and sensations within the body as you breathe in and out. When you find your mind wandering, simply acknowledge the distracting thoughts and gently draw your focus back to your breath. Don't stop intruding thoughts. The more you attempt to push them away, the more power they gain over you. Instead simply acknowledge these thoughts, let them live briefly in your consciousness and gently release them.

Similarly, practice more mindfulness in everyday acts such as eating, walking, and driving. Tune in to the present with greater awareness and appreciation. Focus your awareness on the act in a more purposeful and non-judgmental manner.

Meditation and mindfulness keep your craving for "instant fixes" in check. We yearn for immediate gratification without worrying about the consequences of our actions. Long term rewards become hazy when the temptation of instant fulfillment looks endearingly at us. A consistent and disciplined practice of meditation strengthens your resolve. It builds your resistance towards taking rash, impulsive decisions. You become more purposeful, directed and mindful of the impact of your decisions.

Conclusion

Thank you for downloading this book.

I hope it was able to help you learn more about habits, self-discipline, and practical strategies through which you can start implementing good habits in your life right away to become the best version of yourself. I have included innumerable action plans, practical strategies, and proven techniques for developing greater self-discipline and more effective habits in life, which can help you accomplish all your goals.

The book is packed with plenty of time management, goal writing, productivity-boosting, anti-procrastination, and other valuable self-discipline hacks that will help you get on the effective habits and self-discipline lane straightaway.

The next step is to take action. A person who does not read is as good as a person who cannot read. Similarly, knowledge without action is pointless. One cannot achieve self-discipline only by reading about it and feeling great. You have to go out there and put it into practice to make it work! You have to sweat it out and give it your all to emerge a winner!

Lastly, if you enjoyed reading the book, please take some time to share your views and post a review. It'd be greatly appreciated.

Here's to a more rewarding, fulfilling, accomplished, and self-discipline filled life!

www.ingramcontent.com/pod-product-compliance
Lightning Source LLC
Chambersburg PA
CBHW070233180526
45158CB00001BA/461